MY GUIDE TO UNDERSTANDING

ISLAM

- VOL. 3 -

MY GUIDE TO UNDERSTANDING

ISLAM

- VOL. 3 -

YUSUF KARAGÖL

NEW JERSEY • LONDON • FRANKFURT • CAIRO • JAKARTA

TUGHRA
BOOKS

New Jersey

Published by Tughra Books
345 Clifton Ave., Clifton,
NJ, 07011, USA

www.tughrabooks.com

Library of Congress Cataloging-in-Publication Data Available

ISBN: 978-1-59784-343-0

Printed by
Imak Ofset, Istanbul - Turkey

TABLE OF CONTENTS

CHAPTER 1

CHAPTER 2

CHAPTER 3

CHAPTER 4

CHAPTER 8

CHAPTER 9

CHAPTER 10

ADDITIONAL TOPICS

CHAPTER 1

THE IMPORTANCE
OF READING

Reading Brings Us Closer to Our Lord

A curious and sincere reader increases his knowledge, understands his own poverty and weakness, sees that he is in fact nothing, and realizes that all the power and strength lies with God. Such reading brings the person closer to Him. The Qur'anic verse, "*Are they ever equal, those who know and those who do not know?*" (az-Zumar 39:9) points out the superiority of readers.

Let us see how our noble Prophet explains the way reading brings humans closer to God: "At home the candle tears through the darkness and shows things, by alighting beneficial knowledge, illuminating the heart, raising the curtains, moving the person away from *masiwa* (everything other than Allah), it brings him closer to Allah, may His glory be exalted."

The Messenger of Allah, peace and blessings be upon him, said "Scholars are the inheritors of the Prophets" (*Sunan at-Tirmidhi*). Indeed, the righteous and devoted scholars, who in terms of knowledge and morals are the inheritors of the Prophets, are certainly the means of guidance and prosperity.

Reading works that will make one closer to God Almighty is praiseworthy. Even more commendable is to take one's reading beyond theory by seeking ways to bring one's knowledge into practice, for one's servanthood depends on daily improving one's performance. The essence of *ilm* (knowledge) is practice, and its purpose is to come closer to the All-Compassionate.

Our noble Prophet stated, "He who is asked about knowledge (of religion) and conceals it, will be bridled with a bridle of fire on the Day of Resurrection."

Human being is like a perfect ever-renewing machine, and a marvelous and ever-changing palace. He need constant renewal through reading, contemplation, prayer, and good deeds. In Sufi terms, to become *al-insan al-kamil*, the perfect soul or the universal human being, is the real meaning and purpose of existence. Perfection can be attained through reading, but reading alone does not suffice. The knowledge obtained through reading must be supported by righteous deeds.

BELIEF

The Monk in the Monastery

The Caliph Umar, may Allah be pleased with him, together with his friends, was passing before a monastery when he saw a monk with his long gray beard and who was also very old. Suddenly Umar gave way at the knees. He sat and started to cry at once. His friends were surprised and asked each other: "What happened?"

Yet, none of them knew the answer. One of them asked the caliph: "O Umar, what has made you cry so much?"

He, pointing to the monk in the monastery, said, "That monk is almost at the last steps of his life, yet, he still does not know the Messenger of Allah, that's why I cry."

The Caliph was crying for someone who he did not even recognize. He was crying because the monk couldn't find out the reality which was shining so evidently for anyone who was not prejudiced.

After all, it could have been no one other than Umar and the ones like him, who could donate half of their property without even thinking a second, and who could also cry for someone in a profound need of finding the truth of life.

The Second Word

In the Name of God, the All-Merciful, the All-Compassionate.

"*Those who believe in the Unseen*" (al-Baqarah 2:2).

If you wish to understand how to enjoy great contentment and blessing through belief, and how to experience fulfillment and ease, consider the following parable: Two people travel for both pleasure and business. The first one is conceited and pessimistic, and so ends up in what he considers a most wicked country. He sees himself surrounded by poor and hopeless people tormented by bullies and living ruined lives. He sees the same grievous, painful situation wherever he goes, as if the whole country were a house of mourning. In order not to feel this painful situation, he finds no other way out than becoming drunk. Everyone seems to him to be an enemy and foreigner. He has awful visions of corpses and orphans, and his soul is plunged into torment.

The second person, a God-serving, decent, and fair-minded man, goes to a country that he considers quite excellent. Seeing a universal festival, he finds joy and happiness in every corner, and a house for remembering God overflowing with rapture. Everyone is a loving friend, even a relative, to him. He sees the celebrations of a general discharge from duties accompanied by cries of good wishes and thanks. Hearing a drum and a band for enlisting soldiers with happy calls of "God is the All-Great" and "There is no deity but God," he becomes happy at his own joy and that of others. He enjoys a comfortable trade and thanks God.

When he returns after some while, he meets the other man, understands his situation and says: "You've become crazy. The bad and ugly things you see come from and reflect your inner world. You imagine laughter to be weeping, and discharge from duties to be sack and pillage. Come to your senses and clean your heart, so that this inauspicious veil will be raised from your eyes and you may see the truth. This is an orderly, prosperous, and civilized country with a powerful, compassionate, and just ruler. So things cannot be as you see or think." The man comes to his senses and is full of regret: "Yes, I've really gone crazy because of all those intoxicants. Thank you. May God be pleased with you for rescuing me from such a hellish state."

O my soul! The first person represents an unbeliever or a heedless sinner who sees this world as a place of general mourning, all living things as weeping orphans due to the pain of separation and decay, people and animals as lonely and uncivilized creatures cut down by death, and great masses (mountains and oceans) as terrible corpses without souls. His unbelief and misguidance breed great anxieties that torture him.

The second person believes in and affirms God Almighty. He sees the world as a place where people glorify, praise and exalt Him, a practice arena for people and animals, and an examination hall for people and jinn. Animals and humanity are demobilized so that after death believers can travel in spiritual enjoyment to the other world—for this world needs a new generation to populate and work in it.

All animals and people enter this world for a reason. All living things are as soldiers or officials, happy with their appointed task. The sound we hear is their praise and glorifying as they begin, or their pleasure while working, or their thanksgiving as they finish. Believers see all things as obedient servants, friendly officials, a lovable book of their All-Munificent Master and All-Compassionate Owner.

Many more such beautiful, sublime, and pleasurable truths arise from belief. This is because belief bears the seed of what is, in effect, a Touba tree of Paradise, whereas unbelief contains the seed of a Zaqqum tree of Hell. Safety and well-being are found only in Islam (submission to God) and belief. Therefore, always thank God, saying: "Praise be to God for Islam and perfect belief." (Nursi, *The Words*, "The Second Word").

QUESTIONS

1) The Messenger of Allah implied scholars are the inheritors of whom?

    A) the Prophets   C) the Companions

    B) the *mujtahids*   D) the caliphs

2) "He who is asked about knowledge (of religion) and conceals it, will be bridled with a bridle of fire on the Day of Resurrection." What category does this sentence belong to?

    A) verse   C) *hadith*

    B) adage   D) expression

3) "_____ is like a perfect ever-renewing machine, and a marvelous and ever-changing palace." Which of the following should be in the blank place?

    A) Air   C) An atom

    B) A human being   D) An element

4) Which caliph who, when passing in front of a monastery and seeing an old monk not believing, burst into tears?

    A) Abu Bakr   C) Uthman

    B) Umar   D) Ali

5) In which *surah* of the Qur'an is the verse, "*Those who believe in the Unseen*"?

    A) Ya-Sin   C) al-Fatiha

    B) al-Fath   D) al-Baqarah

6) "Safety and well-being are found only in _____ and _____." Which words best fill in the blanks?

    A) Islam, belief   C) Hereafter, belief

    B) Islam, good manners   D) Hereafter, good manners

7) Which group is described as "lonely and uncivilized creatures cut down by death" in the parable of the Second Word?

A) the universe and people

B) people and animals

C) inanimate objects

D) the universe and animals

8) "This is because belief bears the seed of what is, in effect, a _____ of Paradise, whereas unbelief contains the seed of a _____ of Hell." Which words best fill in the blanks?

A) Touba tree, Zaqqum tree

B) Zaqqum tree, Touba tree

C) Touba tree, Zahdari

D) Zaqqum tree, Zahdari

CHAPTER 2

BELIEF AND WORSHIP

The eminent scholar Said Nursi (1877–1960) wrote about the truths and essentials of the Islamic faith, the meaning and importance of worship, morality, and the meaning of existence, and he was very original in his approach. Here is a section from his *Risale-i Nur* (Treatise of Light) Collection:

The following is a brief indication of one of the thousands of the universal proofs of the pillar of belief in God, many of which, together with explanations, can be found in the *Risale-i Nur*.

In Kastamonu some high-school students asked me: "Tell us about our Creator, for our teachers do not speak of Him." I replied as follows:

All of the sciences you study speak continuously of God, the Creator, in its own tongue, and makes Him known. Do not listen to your teachers; listen to them.

For example, a well-equipped, well-designed pharmacy has many medicines and pills, composed of different, precisely-measured components. This indicates, without a doubt, to the existence of an extremely skillful and learned pharmacist. In the same way, the pharmacy of the earth is stocked with countless life-giving cures and medicines. Through the science of medicine, even the blind can know the All-Wise One of Majesty Who is the Pharmacist of the largest pharmacy of the earth.

Let us use another example. A wonderful factory that produces thousands of different cloths woven from a simple material indicates without a doubt the existence of a manufacturer and a skillful mechanical engineer. Similarly, the factory of the Lord, which we call the earth, has countless parts, and each part possesses hundreds of thousands of machines. Without a doubt, the factory that is the earth makes known, through the science of engineering, the existence of its Manufacturer and Owner.

Another example is a shop that has a well-organized storage place for numerous varieties of provisions brought there from hundreds of different places. The very existence of the shop indicates in turn the existence of a shop owner who prepares, stores, and distributes those provisions. Now the earth on which we live may be seen as a huge storehouse of mercy or a Divine vessel which traverses a vast orbit each year, housing innumerable species which require different foods: as it passes through the seasons on its journey, it fills spring, which is like a huge wagon, with a great variety of provisions and brings them to all the living creatures whose sustenance was exhausted during the winter. This storage depot, which is the earth, surely indicates, through the science of economics which you are studying, the existence of the Owner, Manager, and Organizer of this depot that is the earth and makes Him loved.

Or imagine, for example, an army that consists of numerous tribes and nations, each one requiring unique provisions, weapons, uniforms, drills, and demobilization. If its miracle-working commander meets all their needs on his own, without forgetting or confusing any of them, surely the army and its camp will serve as an indication of this commander's existence and make him appreciated. Similarly, every spring a single Commander-in-Chief provides a newly recruited army of countless animal and plant species with uniforms, rations, weapons, training, and demobilizations in a perfect and regular fashion. He forgets nothing and does not become confused. This Divine army of spring indicates, through military science, the existence of that most attentive and sensible Ruler of the earth, its Lord, Administrator and All-Holy Commander, and makes Him loved, praised, glorified, and acclaimed.

Or imagine a magnificent city illuminated by millions of mobile electric lamps with an inexhaustible fuel and power source. Such a set-up would evidently point to the talent of a wonder-working artisan and extraordinarily skillful electrician who makes the lamps, establishes the power source, and provides the fuel. And it would cause others to admire and congratulate this electrician.

Now many of the lamps—the planets and the stars—which adorn the roof of the palace that is the world, in the city that is the universe, are a thousand times larger than the earth and move with an amazing speed. Yet despite their rapidity, they move most precisely without colliding with one another; they are not extinguished, nor do they run out of fuel. The science of astronomy, which you study, tells us that our sun, which is like a lamp or a stove in the guesthouse of the All-Merciful, is hundreds of thousands of times larger than the earth and several billion years old. To keep burning each day, it needs as much oil as there are seas on the earth, as much coal as there are mountains, or as many logs and pieces of wood as exist on ten earths.

It is clear, then, that such lamps indicate with their fingers of light the existence of an infinite Power and Sovereignty Which, in turn, illuminates the sun and other similar stars without oil, wood, or coal, allowing them to travel at great speed without colliding with one another or being extinguished. Thus, the science of electricity and the testimony of those radiant stars indubitably indicate the existence of the Sovereign, Illuminator, Director, and Creator of the greatest light exhibition of the universe, and make Him loved, glorified, and adored.

Now imagine a marvelous book. Within each line of that book, another, smaller book has been written, and within each word, a whole chapter—a *surah*—has been inscribed with a fine pen. This book is most meaningful and expressive, and all of its topics corroborate each other. Such a book shows as clearly as daylight that it must be the product of a particular artist, who is possessed of extraordinary perfections, arts, and skills. It makes us appreciate the author and call down God's blessings upon him.

What is true of the book in the example is true of the vast book that is the universe. For example, we see with our own eyes a pen inscribing on the page of the earth hundreds of thousands of plants and animal species, each one of which is like an entire volume in itself. And they are inscribed all together, one within the other, without error or confusion; they are inscribed with such perfection and precision that an ode is compressed in a single word, like a tree, and an entire book is to be found within a point that is a seed. However much vaster and more perfect and meaningful than the book in the example mentioned above is this infinitely meaningful compendium that is the universe, this embodied 'macro-Qur'an,' in every word of which there are numerous instances of wisdom, to that degree—through the natural sciences that you study, it makes known the Inscriber and Author of this book of the universe with His infinite Perfections. Proclaiming "God is the All-Great," it makes Him known; declaring His sacredness with "All-Glorified is God," it describes Him; and praising Him with such expressions as "All praise and gratitude are for God," it makes Him loved.

Indeed, through its extensive measure, its particular mirror, its far-reaching view, and its searching and instructive perspectives, each of the hundreds of sciences makes the All-Majestic Creator of the universe known with His Names, Attributes and Perfections.

It is in order to elucidate the evidence explained above, which constitute a most convincing and magnificent proof of Divine Unity, that the miraculous Qur'an frequently describes our Creator in terms such as "the Lord of the heavens and the earth" and "the Creator of the heavens and the earth".

I told the students all of this and they accepted and affirmed it, saying: "Endless thanks be to God, for we have received a true and sacred lesson. May God be pleased with you."

I added as follows:

A human being is a living machine subject to many sorrows and capable of knowing many pleasures. Although totally impotent, we have infinite physical and spiritual enemies. Although completely destitute, we have infinite internal and external needs, and we suffer continuously from the blows of gradual decay and separation. But if, through belief and worship, we can establish a connection with the All-Majestic Sovereign, we will find a source of support against all of our enemies and a source of help for all of our needs. Everyone takes pride in the honor and rank of those in high places with whom they enjoy a connection. Given this fact, if one establishes a connection through belief with the infinitely Powerful and Compassionate Sovereign; if one enters His service through worship and, by so doing, changes the sentence of execution at the appointed hour of death into a most welcome acquittal and discharge, imagine the pride, joy, and contentment they will feel.

To the calamity-stricken prisoners I repeat what I said to the school-boys: Those who recognize and obey Him are prosperous, even if they are in prison, while those who forget Him are like wretched prisoners even if they live in palaces.

Once a wronged but fortunate man—fortunate on account of his belief and ensuing martyrdom—said to the wretched wrongdoers who were executing him: "I am not being executed; rather, I have been discharged from my duties and am going forward to eternal happiness. However, I can now see that you are condemned to eternal punishment; this suffices as my revenge upon you." And saying "There is no deity but God," he died a happy man.

All-Glorified are You! We have no knowledge save what You have taught us. Surely you are the All-Knowing, the All-Wise. (Nursi, *The Rays*, "The Eleventh Ray", "The Sixth Matter").

SALAH (DAILY PRAYERS)

How Were the Daily Prayers of Our Prophet?

Our noble Prophet was fond of Prayer, because in his words, *Salah* was the pillar of Islam and the light of his eyes. *Salah* was like the washing of the body. Like bathing five times a day in a river would cleanse one from dirt, *wudu* and *Salah* cleanse the believer from faults and sins, from overt and covert ugliness. Our beloved Prophet performed his Prayers in perfect servanthood, and he taught his Companions to do the same. It was conveyed in that way, from generation to generation, to the present day. Believers strive to acquire the same consciousness of servanthood, and aim to perform it like our noble Prophet did.

The Prayer is the most vital duty of servanthood. In a *hadith* narrated by Abu Hurayra, our beloved Prophet says: "The first of man's deeds for which he will be called to account on the Day of Resurrection will be *Salah*. If it is found to be perfect, he will be safe and successful; but if it is incomplete, he will be unfortunate and a loser."

In this world, the sign of Islam and servanthood is *Salah*; the first subject in the next is *Salah*. This fact is expressed in a *hadith*: "On the Day of Judgment the first thing a servant is going to be taken to task for will be his obligatory Prayers. If he did not perform them, then it will be said: Go and check if he has some extra voluntary Prayers. If he does, the shortcomings of the obligatory Prayers are made up by these voluntary Prayers and forgiven."

The Companions observed carefully the way our greatest guide, Prophet Muhammad, peace and blessings be upon him, performed his *Salah*. It is said that the noble Messenger kept the same composure and seriousness in his bowing, prostration, sitting between prostrations, greeting at the end of the Prayer, and leaving the place of Prayer.

As our dear Prophet performed his Prayers fully and completely, he asks his community to show the same sensitive gravity: "Observe my Prayers, and do the same." The Companions obeyed this advice and showed thoughtfulness and composure in their *Salah*.

Wasila ibn Mabad narrated: "I have seen the Messenger of Allah praying. When he went to *ruku* (bowing), his back would become straight, so much so that if you poured water on it, it would remain without sliding to either side."

Our dear Prophet paid rapt attention to the rules of the Prayer, and he cautioned those who were more careless. Ali ibn Shayban narrated: "We made a congregation for the Messenger of Allah and we prayed behind him. Then he saw a man who did not pray according to its rules. The *ruku* of the man who prayed was not proper. When he was finished with the Prayer, the Messenger of Allah said, 'O Muslims! The Prayer is not valid if a man does not bring his backbone to rest while bowing and prostrating.' The Messenger of Allah did not allow even the slightest negligence or fault in Prayer. He did not approve of those who hurried to pass over a part (*rukn*) of the Prayer or who prayed half-heartedly, and considered a shortcoming in Prayer the same as stealing. He used to say, "The worst of thieves is the one who steals his Prayer: He does not do bowing or prostrating properly."

QUESTIONS

1) "Some high-school students asked me: "Tell us about our Creator, for our teachers do not speak of Him." The high school students who complained about their teachers were located in which city?

    A) Isparta   C) Afyon

    B) Denizli   D) Kastamonu

2) Which example below was not mentioned as an answer to the question of the high school students in "The Sixth Matter"?

    A) the pharmacy of this world

    B) a marvelous factory

    C) thousands of kinds of fabulous provisions

    D) coincidental (chance) events in the universe

3) "Those who recognize and obey Him are _____, even if they are in prison, while those who forget Him are like _____ prisoners even if they live in palaces."

    Which best fill in the blanks?

    A) unhappy, absentminded

    B) unhappy, happy

    C) prosperous, wretched

    D) absentminded, fortunate

4) Which devotion is our most vital duty as a servant?

    A) Fasting   C) Hajj

    B) *Zakah*   D) *Salah*

5) Our noble Prophet says: "The first of man's deeds for which he will be called to account on the Day of Resurrection will be *Salah*. If it is found to be perfect, he will be safe and successful; but if it is incomplete, he will be unfortunate and a loser." Which Companion of the Messenger of Allah narrated this *hadith*?

A) Abu Hurayra   C) Umar
B) Abu Bakr   D) Zayd

6) "We made a congregation for the Messenger of Allah and we prayed behind him. Then he saw a man who did not pray according to its rules. The *ruku* of the man who prayed was not proper. When he was finished with the Prayer, the Messenger of Allah said, 'O Muslims! The Prayer is not valid if a man does not bring his backbone to rest while bowing and prostrating.'" Which Companion narrated this story?

     A) Wasila ibn Ma'bad   C) Abu Hurayra
     B) Ali ibn Shayban   D) Ali ibn Abu Talib

7) Our dear Prophet did not allow even the slightest fault or negligence in Prayer. He did not permit hurrying or carelessness in event one small part of the Prayer, considering any deficiency in Prayer as theft: "The worst of thieves is the one who steals his Prayer: He does not do bowing or _____ properly." Which best fills in the blank?

     A) *qiyam*   C) prostrating
     B) *takbir*   D) *ruku*

CHAPTER 3

DIVINE DESTINY
AND SUPPLICATION

Who Is the Most Blessed among Human Beings?

One day when our noble Prophet was sitting in the mosque, a man walked in and asked:

"Who is the most blessed amongst human beings?"

The Messenger of Allah replied: "The most blessed is the one who enjoins the good and forbids the evil, recites the Qur'an a lot, fears God and visits his parents and relatives." The *hadith* explains that in order to become a believer whom God and His Messenger is pleased with, one needs to convey the message of God. This duty is more blessed than secluding into one corner. If this was not the case, our Prophet would have refrained from society and stayed in his house at all times to offer his Prayers day and night. Therefore, if we wish to be amongst the most blessed people then we should use every opportunity to explain about our Lord to others.

By guiding other people to the right path we get the chance to earn rewards as much as the number of people who have embraced our faith. Let us explain the issue more meticulously: For instance, a believer has encouraged his friend to perform good deeds. In such a case, the same amount of spiritual rewards earned by the friend who performs good deeds will also be earned by the person who has guided him, without any decrease in the rewards. Our noble Prophet states: "A person, who causes something good or teaches a good deed to someone else, will be considered as if he has performed this deed himself."

As it is clear by the *hadith*, taking even the smallest step on this path earns great rewards hence it signifies the importance of performing "enjoining good and forbidding evil."

Divine Determining and Decree

Qadar (Divine Determining) comes from a root word meaning to measure, to form and to shape. Allah the Almighty knows and decides all things that would take place for all eternity, including their time and place, their qualities and attributes. The literal meaning of *Qada* (Decree) denotes commandment, judgment and creation.

The All-Majestic Creator has infinite knowledge. He knows the past, present and future altogether. He is not limited by the past, present or future. He knows everything, from the particles to the starts, from the Corporeal or Visible Realm to World of the Unseen. If a line extended from past-eternity to post- eternity, it is He Who determines the place of all things, including all of their attributes, deciding and determining with His infinite Knowledge and Will. He creates everything according to His Knowledge.

Knowing something does not mean bringing that thing into existence. If we plan one thousand buildings, or design the feasibility of hundreds of factories, none would exist merely because we have them in our minds. There must be a will and power to act. Without will and power, the buildings and factories exist only in our minds.

Qadar is a kind of knowledge, and that knowledge is subject to the known. In other words, a thing is known as it is, or as it will be. Otherwise, the known is not subject to the knowledge. The

All-Knowing knows what we will do, and in what ways we will use our will, and makes His determinations according to His all-encompassing Knowledge.

Divine Knowledge is not limited with time or space. His Knowledge envelops all things, with all their aspects. Allah is All-Merciful and All-Wise, and His Decree is done according to His Infinite and Perfect Knowledge.

Belief Requires Prayer

Belief requires prayer for attainment and perfection, and our essence needs it. God Almighty says: *"Say (O Muhammad): 'My Lord would not concern Himself with you but for your prayer'"* (25:77), and: *"Pray to Me and I will answer you"* (40:60).

Question: If you say that you pray so many times but that your prayers are unanswered, despite the assurance given in the above verse, the answer would be as follows:

An answered prayer does not necessarily mean its acceptance. There is an answer for every prayer. However, accepting the prayer and giving what is requested depends upon the All-Mighty's Wisdom. For example, a sick child asks a doctor for a certain medicine. The doctor will give either what is asked for or something better, or he will not give anything. It all depends upon how the medicine will affect the child. Similarly the All-Mighty, Who is the All-Just and Omnipresent, answers His servants' prayer and changes their loneliness into the pleasure of His company. But His answer does not depend on the individual's fancies; rather, according to His Wisdom, He gives what is requested, what is better, or nothing at all. Moreover, prayer is a form of worship and worship is rewarded mainly in the Hereafter. Worldly needs and purposes are only causes or occasions for prayer. For example, praying for rain is a kind of worship occasioned by the lack of rain. If rain is the prayer's only aim, the prayer is unacceptable, for it is not sincere or intended to please God and obtain His approval. Sunset determines the time for the evening Prayer, while solar and lunar eclipses occasion two particular kinds of worship. Since such eclipses—the veiling of two luminous signs of day and night—are two means of manifesting Divine Majesty, the All-Mighty calls His servants to perform a form of worship—the Prayer of Eclipse—particular to these occasions. This Prayer has nothing to do with causing the eclipse to end, for this is known already through astronomical calculations. Similarly, drought and other calamities are occasions certain kinds of prayer. At such times, we best realize our impotence and so feel the need to take refuge in the high Presence of the Absolutely Powerful One through prayer and supplication.

If a calamity is not lifted despite many prayers, we should not say that the prayer has not been accepted. Rather, we should say that the time for prayer has not yet ended. If God removes the calamity because of His endless Grace and Munificence, this is light upon light, profit upon profit, and marks the end of the special occasion for prayer.

Praying is a mystery of servanthood to God through worship. Worship is done solely to please God and for His Sake. We should affirm and display our poverty and weakness, and seek refuge with Him through prayer. We must not interfere in His Lordship, but rather let God do as He wills. We must rely on His Wisdom and not accuse His Mercy.

Every creature offers its unique praise and worship to God. What reaches the Court of God from the universe is prayer.

One kind of prayer is that which is done through the tongue of potential. Plants pray through the tongue of their potential to achieve a full form and manifest certain Divine Names.

Another kind of prayer is expressed in the tongue of natural needs. All living beings ask the Absolutely Generous One to meet their vital needs, as they cannot do so on their own.

Yet another kind of prayer is done in the tongue of complete helplessness. A living creature in straitened circumstances takes refuge in its Unseen Protector with a genuine supplication and turns to its All-Compassionate Lord. These three kinds of prayer are always acceptable, unless somehow impeded.

The fourth type of prayer is the one done by humanity. This type falls into two categories: active and by disposition, and verbal and with the heart. For example, acting in accordance with causes or fulfilling the prerequisites is an active prayer. We try to gain God's approval by complying with causes or fulfilling the prerequisites, for causes alone or the fulfillment of prerequisites cannot produce the result—only God can do that. For example, plowing the soil is an active prayer, for this means knocking at the door of the treasury of God's Mercy. Such a prayer is usually acceptable, for it is an application to the Divine Name the All-Generous.

The second type of prayer of humanity, done with the tongue and the heart, is the ordinary one. This means that we ask God from the heart for something we cannot reach. Its most important aspect and finest and sweetest fruit is that we know that God hears us, is aware of our heart's contents, that His Power extends everywhere, that He can satisfy every desire, and that He comes to our aid out of mercy for our weakness and inadequacy.

And so, O helpless and poor person. Never abandon prayer, for it is the key to the Treasury of Mercy and the means of gaining access to the Infinite Power. Hold on to it. Ascend to the highest rank of humanity and, as creation's most favored and superior member, include the whole universe's prayer in your prayer. Say, on behalf of all beings: *From You alone do we seek help* (1:5), and become a beautiful pattern for creation. (Nursi, *The Words*, "The Twenty-Third Word").

Medicine Has Been Found for the Illness of Sin

Bayazid Bastami (d. 804–874), a well-known Sufi, was passing in front of an insane asylum one day. He saw that a servant of the asylum was hitting something with a pestle and he asked: "What are you doing?"

Servant replied: "This is an insane asylum. I am making medicine for the crazy."

"Can you recommend a medicine for my illness?" Bastami asked.

"What is your illness?"

"My illness is the illness of sin. I commit a lot of sins."

"I know nothing about the illness of sin. I am making medicine for the crazy…"

A crazy person (!) who heard the conversation from behind bars said to Bayazid Bastami: "Come here grandfather, come here! I will tell you the cure for your illness."

Drawing near to the madman, Bayazid Bastami asked: "What is the cure for my trouble?"

The madman (!) recommended this medicine: "Mix a repentance root with a leaf of penitence. Ground it in the mortar of the heart with the pestle of *tawhid* (the Oneness and Unity of God), pass it through a sieve of mercy, knead it with tears and bake it in the oven of love. Eat a large amount morning and evening. Then you will see that nothing remains of your illness."

Learning this good medicine, Bastami said: "This is really strange! So they brought you here as a madman."

Then he left.

This medicine is still worthy of recommendation to those with the illness of sin. In other words, the formula still works.

QUESTIONS

1) One day when our noble Prophet was at the pulpit in the Prophet's Mosque, a man came and asked the Messenger, "Who is the most blessed amongst human beings?" Which of the following was not in the answer the Messenger gave?

    A) the one who enjoins the good and forbids the evil

    B) the one who recites the Qur'an a lot

    C) the one who works hard and earns more

    D) the one who fears God and visits his parents and relatives

2) What term—which could be rendered as measuring, shaping, deeming, forming—means Allah's knowing the time and places of things taking place from past-eternity until post-eternity, as well as their qualities in advance, and willing it to be.

    A) *Qadar*   C) *Jihad*

    B) *Qada*   D) *Ikhlas*

3) The sentence, "My Lord would not concern Himself with you but for your prayer" could be categorized as which of the following?

    A) *Hadith*   C) Adage

    B) Verse   D) Expression

4) Who is the spiritual guide mentioned in the phrase, "The cure for the disease of sin is discovered"?

    A) Mawlana Jalaluddin Rumi

    B) Bediüzzaman Said Nursi

    C) Bayazid Bastami

    D) Uways al-Qarani

5) "Mix a repentance root with a leaf of penitence. Ground it in the mortar of the heart with the pestle of *tawhid*, pass it through a sieve of mercy, knead it with tears and bake it in the oven of

love. Eat a large amount morning and evening. Then you will see that nothing remains of your illness." This cure would be appropriate for which of the following diseases?

A) The disease of sin

B) Stress

C) Psychological diseases

D) Heart disease

6) "Prayer is a form of _____, which is rewarded mainly in the Hereafter." Which word best fills the blank?

A) planning

B) imagining

C) crying

D) worship

7) The literal meaning of _____ is commandment, judgment and creation, the creation of everything ordained in past-eternity as Allah decreed. Which word best fills the blank?

A) *Qadar*

B) *Qada*

C) *Jihad*

D) *Ikhlas*

CHAPTER 4

BEDİÜZZAMAN SAİD NURSİ: AN ISLAMIC SCHOLAR WITH PURIFIED MIND AND HEART

The Reason for His Cause Was Commandment, and Its Result Was the Pleasure of Allah

In Islam *hikmah* (wisdom) is very significant. The universe is created with purpose, measure and consistency. The one who seeks mysteries will raise the curtain, and find his owner.

Order and commandment are more important than purpose and utility. *Amr* (order, commandment) is preference of the Sultan over any gain. Order is to understand the smallness of the self and the absolute Divine Essence. We cannot squeeze the oceans into a small pool; we must not relate to "reason" alone the unknowable number of purposes of the One who possesses infinite knowledge. Doing something solely because it is His command is where one's pleasure lies.

Even though Bediüzzaman (a title of Said Nursi, meaning "the Wonder of the Age") looks at matters through the lens of a sound reason, searching for the religious or Divine wisdom, he always lived within that courtesy, never becoming a prisoner of his own reason and mind. His feet were never entangled with his own shadow. It was obvious that his every word came from beyond the cage of his own body. One must listen to the voice that comes from the beyond, i.e. the Divine revelation; it is the necessary consequence of belief and sincerity.

Throughout the *Risale-i Nur*, a detailed exposition of the matter was made: The soul of devotion is sincerity. Sincerity is devotion because it was commanded. If some other reason is the cause for devotion, the devotion is invalid. The benefits or wisdom is perhaps a reason for preference, but not the cause.

Bediüzzaman Said Nursi brings to mind the sincerity of Jalaluddin Khawarzmshah:

> When [he] was going to war, his ministers said to him, "You will be victorious; God Almighty will make you victorious." He replied, "I am charged with striving in God's cause. I cannot interfere in God's judgment or way of acting. It is His judgment whether He will make me victorious or not." Due to his understanding of the true meaning of submission to God, he was wonderfully and unexpectedly victorious on many occasions.

In the treatise on *ijtihad*, Bediüzzaman Said Nursi explains how order is beyond wisdom. During travel the Prayers are shortened not because of the difficulties, but because it is ordered. He explained that although when there are other difficulties, the Prayers are not shortened; they are shortened during travel even when there is no difficulty.

He presented his service as obeying the order of dissemination of the truth, with the sole purpose of gaining the pleasure of Allah, and he considered other reasons as invalid. The devoted people must prefer the pleasure of their Lord. The loyal servant prefers the pleasure of his Master to his own interests.

In order not to overshadow his cause, he tried to accomplish his duty in the best way, and he did not base it on acceptance or rejection by the public. The sole aim of the heart should be the pleasure and consent of the All-Merciful.

To further elucidate the courtesy in this matter, in *The Gleams* he says:

> The true success is not having a vast following but rather is gaining God's good pleasure. What do you imagine yourself to be that by thinking, "Let everyone listen to me," you forget your own duty and interfere in God's Will? It is only God Who, if He wills, will make people accept you and gather around you. So mind your own duty, and do not interfere in God's Will.

This lesson is enough for the people of comprehension and understanding. Devotion and religious services are performed solely because they are ordered. Sentiments such as having a desire for performing wonders, gaining the admiration of the public, and other considerations are deviations from the Straight Path. Because of such tendencies, they cannot expel the fogs in their hearts, they cannot have spiritual satisfaction. Their share is only contempt, to be ridiculed.

Becoming a servant of the Qur'an is the highest position one may aspire to. Bediüzzaman says: "I am the warden of the jewelry store that is the Qur'an. Like a penniless person advertising a rich jeweler's jewelry, I advertise the Qur'an's jewelry."

Here Is the Shepherd's Sincerity!

God protects His servants from misfortunes and calamities based on their *ikhlas* (sincerity). Bediüzzaman asks Truthful Süleyman, who had been giving out tea at that moment, a question: "Süleyman, have you ever entered a jail?"

"I haven't been given that blessing, master," Truthful Süleyman replies. On top of this Bediüzzaman says, "Due to your devotion and sincerity, that duty has been removed from you."

"You should know that all your power lies in sincerity and truth," Bediüzzaman says. "The prayers of those who turn towards God with *ikhlas* will be accepted. Those who carry out their work with *ikhlas* will be successful." A story from M. Necati Sepetçioğlu's book called *Anadolu Efsaneleri* (Anatolian Legends) expresses this truth very nicely:

> In a city in Anatolia when an alcoholic who had taken a philosophical attitude on life died, the imam and the city's people left him without a funeral prayer. The man's wife took her deceased husband onto her shoulders and began carrying him towards the mountains. She asked for help from a shepherd she then came upon. They bury her husband together. "Can you also make a prayer?" The woman asks the shepherd. The shepherd says he doesn't know any prayers but he raises his hands and quietly mutters one or two sentences and finishes his prayer.
>
> The woman then returns home to her village and home. The leaders of the village, in fact the imam himself, see the man in his dreams in a scene of Paradise. This news spread throughout the village. Everyone began searching for the reason behind this. Finally they decided to ask the woman: "Where did you bury your husband, and how? This is what we've heard!" The woman explained everything in its complete simplicity: "I didn't do anything! Whatever it is, it's from that shepherd's prayer!"
>
> They go to the shepherd. "You apparently made a prayer after you buried the man; what did you say?" they asked. "O God! I fed the people that passed through here with my food and let them drink from my milk, thinking they were God's guests and Your guests. I am also sending a guest, host him according to Your Glory, O God!" the shepherd replied.
>
> This is the shepherd's *ikhlas*! Sincerity brings near what is far away, makes many out of little, and makes important what is unimportant.

He Was Not Greedy, but Contented

One of the most distinctive attributes of Bediüzzaman is *istighna* (dignified contentment). He lived as a role model of content-ment. All who went to visit him took away the memory of an incident that demonstrated this. The man who asked from Allah whatever he wanted to ask, who knocked on the door of the Divine Names, was practically bashful about expecting anything from his fellow creatures. On the rope where his Lord hung various gifts, he saw the Hand of Mercy, and when he saw a blessing, he did not forget the One giving it.

When his student Hulusi sent a gift, Bediüzzaman said to him, "You sent me a gift, and thus will cause me to break a very important principle. I do not mean that I will refuse your gift, as I refused that of my brother Abdülmecid and my nephew Abdur-rahman, for you are my brother-in-religion, more advanced in reli-gion and in serving it, and more after my own heart. Therefore I accept your gift for the first and last time and explain why, as a rule, I do not accept gifts."

He made an exception, and when he related this incident he explained his principle: "Earlier in my life, I avoided being put under obligation because I would rather be dead than indebted. I have not renounced this principle, although I have suffered great hardship and difficulty... I prefer a piece of dry, stale bread and a robe with many patches, which keeps me away from pre-tense and sycophancy, to having to please others because of the high-quality sweets and clothes they present to me."

This shows the importance he attaches to living with free-dom, without any obligations. In this day and age, greedy human beings sell an insignificant gift for a great price. In order not to lower the value of the lessons others would take from him, from the level of diamonds to that of glass, he avoided his own benefit for the sake of others.

When asked by others how he maintained his life, he said, "Those unfortunate souls do not know the marvelous blessings of a frugal lifestyle." He said the bread he bought for five cents was enough for him for two days. Because they did not know how he was contented with so little, they were cynical. But a man who took fifteen days to eat a loaf of bread, whose worldly possessions could be squeezed into a handkerchief, would never be obligated to anyone.

The man who said, "I can live without bread, but I cannot live without freedom" showed that the way to freedom was not to attack all the food on the table, but through the contentment. The Divine mercy which ordained him to practice this principle did not allow him to eat anything before paying for it.

Since his childhood, he never took anything without giving something in return, and neither collected *zakah* and *sadaqa*. When villagers saw his contentment, they admired him. Although some of them insisted to give some gifts, he did not betray his principles.

When he was in Barla, he paid for everything that was brought to him. Someone had brought pears from his garden to him. He asked one of the students how much it would cost, and in order not to offend him, he took them by paying for them.

One day, Bediüzzaman went to a villager's vineyard. He wanted to pick a few bunches of grapes and give them to Bediüzzaman, and he wanted to pay for them. He said, "No way, what value is it that you should pay for them? I would be honored to give them to you." He took them but then gave him a book as a gift. The villager said Bediüzzaman cried sometimes while looking at a flower with deep contemplation.

Another villager brought apples from his garden, but Bediüzzaman sent his student, Zübeyir Gündüzalp, to the market to learn the price and only accepted them after he had paid. One of his readers used to bring some whipped cream, but Bediüzzaman did not accept it without payment. When he visited his brother Abdülmecid in Konya, he paid for a bowl of soup he offered. His heart cried out and he said, "Brother, for me, too?" He responded, "Please, do not break my principle." His life was full of examples of contentment.

He taught us to ask from Allah alone, not to be obliged to His servants. Especially those who disseminate the truth must follow the example of the Prophets, who said, "*I ask you for no wage; my wage is only due from God*" (Yunus 10:72).

Bediüzzaman, who asked his students to follow this principle, said:

> The mission of the *Risale-i Nur* is material and spiritual altruism. I have sacrificed everything I had, both material and spiritual and I have endured all forms of calamities. I showed endurance and patience to all types of tortures. It is because of this that the truths of faith were distributed to all regions of our nation. And because of this the *Risale-i Nur* raised hundreds of thousands or perhaps millions of students. From now on, they will continue on this path, in the service of faith. They will not detach themselves from my mission of self-sacrifice and given up on everything material and spiritual. They will work only, but only, for the sake of God.

Gaining personal benefits cause problems for those shouldering a spiritual cause. If one of the two individuals gains something more, it may trigger a sense of competition, injure the sense of sincerity, could prevent progress, and could damage the service done.

He provided food for his students and ordered it to be provided, but he directed his attention to this problem, and expressed concern on every occasion. His heroic and self-sacrificing students did not deviate from his principle; they gave and did not take. They did this because they were honored with service to religion; they had already taken the best thing they were supposed to take. Beyond that, there was nothing else worth seeking.

After the death of Bediüzzaman, his student Zübeyir Gündüzalp came to Ankara in order to follow up on a matter relating to his brother and stayed in a hotel. The students of the *Risale-i Nur* invited him to stay with them. He said, "Brothers, I have come to Ankara for a personal matter. Therefore, I could not stay with you. If I had come for *hizmet*, service to faith, then I would stay with you."

The students of the *Risale-i Nur* taught the people about contentment and sacrifice, and spent their wealth while introducing their Lord to people. If this was not the way in those days, when the country and its people had so little, how else could *Risale-i Nur* spread so far, how else could it reach millions?

As for the heroes who went to four corners of the world, sacrificing their youth and wealth, this sublime spirit was obviously inherited from Bediüzzaman and his sincere students.

The Question-Answer Days in Şekerci Han

Bediüzzaman wanted to focus the attention of the sultan, the government, the scholarly class, and the students. So he found a place to stay at the lodging house Şekerci Han and invited the scholars, students, politicians, and soldiers to teachings and debates. He posted the following announcement on the door of his room:

If anyone, religious or irreligious, philosopher or scholar, from school or madrasa, has a question regarding any kind of knowledge or sciences, he may ask me. From you the question, from me the answer...but I shall not question anyone.

This strange proclamation brought a stream of scholars and students to Bediüzzaman from around Istanbul. He did not leave any of their questions unanswered.

On one of his question-answer days, Bediüzzaman came across Sheikh Bahid in a café near Ayasofya (Hagia Sophia). He said of this encounter:

Sheikh Bahid, who was the head scholar of Al-Azhar University, asked the Old Said in the first year of the freedom: "What is your opinion about the freedom movement in the Ottoman government, and what is your opinion of Europe?"

At this, the Old Said said, "The Ottoman government is pregnant with Europe; it will give birth to a state resembling a European state. And Europe is pregnant with Islam; it will give birth to an Islamic country."

That erudite man said, "I affirm what you have said." Then he said to the teachers who had come with him, "I cannot dispute with him and win."

Bediüzzaman believed that these unusual circumstances and experiences in his youth were sent to him by God to prepare him for the great service he would perform in the future.

At first I interpreted the unique happenings throughout my life to be pre-ordained miracles of Ghawth al-Azam (Abdulqadr al-Jilani). Then it became clear that they were miracles attached to the *Risale-i Nur*.

While I was on my way to Istanbul, before the declaration of constitutional monarchy, I came across a couple of books on *Kalam* (Islamic Theology). I carefully examined them. After I arrived in

Istanbul, for no reason I announced that anyone from the scholars, secular schools, or anywhere could ask me any question. To my great surprise, all those who came to debate asked questions about the topics I had studied on the road and which were still in my memory.

Even the questions put to me by the philosophers were on topics I had learnt by heart. In hindsight, it is clear that this marvelous success, well beyond my limitations, this seemingly meaningless manifestation of virtue, was to prepare the groundwork for the *Risale-i Nur* to be accepted by the scholars of Istanbul and to direct their attention to its importance.

The Loudest and Strongest Voice in the Coming Upheavals and Changes

The last days Bediüzzaman spent in Istanbul were also the last days of the Ottoman State, which had been the seat of Islamic rule for 600 years. Every day the news was worse than the day before; at every turn was collapse, decline, and ruin, so that those who loved their country were burning inside. The fortresses of Islam were breached one by one. None could see any hope for the future. On the one hand, some states, which used science and philosophy as weapons, did not even recognize the basic human rights of Muslim communities; the Muslim state, on the other hand, was in bad psychological shape, having long since accepted defeat. What is more, they had fallen prey to the final, most fatal blow: the propaganda of the enemies of Islam who proclaimed that all these defeats sprang from the nature of their religion. But in a time when all hope seemed to have disappeared from the horizons, at least one person was not drawn in by this brainwashing.

Bediüzzaman's reply to those who told him they were exces-
sively grieved over their defeat in World War I was, "I accept the
difficulties that I have suffered, but that which befalls the People
of Islam weighs heavily on me. I feel as though every blow to the
Islamic world strikes my heart first. This is why I am so anguished.
Yet I see a light, and by God's will, this grief will soon be forgotten!" And saying this, he used to smile.

When the light of hope was needed most, Bediüzzaman had
a vision of himself showing that light to the Muslim community.
He described it thus:

> I was searching for a light in that thick darkness. Although I
> could not see the light in the darkness of my waking world, my
> true wakefulness in the dream revealed the light. Leaving aside
> the details, I will only suffice with saying the significant points
> of my dream:
> One Friday night, I entered the world of sleep and dreams
> again. Someone came and said: "A Great Assembly has con-
> vened on the Fate of Islam and has summoned you."
> I went with him and saw a council of enlightened ones, among
> them the Companions of the Prophet as well as those who came
> after the Companions and a representative from the leading
> figures of Islam from each century. I was too shy to go through
> the door. Then one of them said, "O man of the age of calam-
> ity and disasters, you too have a say. Tell us your opinion!"
> Still standing, I said, "If you ask me a question I shall answer."
> So one of them asked, "What will be the end of this defeat?
> And what would have been the end if it had been a victory?"
> I said, "Defeat is not completely evil in every way. Just as
> there is sometimes misfortune in happiness, there can be
> happiness even in disaster. The future felicity of the Islamic
> world will compensate for this loss suffered by this state
> which, since old times, has promoted the way of God, struggled
> for the independence of Muslim peoples, borne the Crescent

flag, and dutifully sacrificed body and soul for the good of the Islamic world.

"In fact, this defeat has in an extraordinary way hastened the day when the Islamic brotherhood we share in this life will awaken and spring into action."

In unison the council commanded, "Explain yourself!"

I said, "Struggles between classes are taking the place of struggles between nations and states. For just as people naturally hate becoming slaves when they lose to their enemies in battles, so they also hate to become hired labor for the enrichment of the upper class. Had we been victorious, we would have been even more severely overwhelmed by this growing class conflict which originates in the hands of our enemies. Whereas, that system—which is pitiless, against the nature of Islam, and against the benefit of the proliferation of the people of faith, and short lived—is likely to break down. If we had won and thus absorbed it, we would have set out on a road that is against the nature and character of Islam. Nothing but harm has come from that exploitative capitalism and aggressive imperialism. And its evil is greater than its good, so it cannot be acceptable in Islam. When humanity awakens, this criminal, dissolute, stubborn, despotic, and spiritually barbaric system is destined to decline. We would have brought this system on ourselves and into Asia."

Since those in the council had wanted an explanation, Bediüzzaman, comparing the two main currents of civilization, said that the modern civilization was built on force rather than truth, and its aim was benefit and self-interest. Therefore its principle is conflict, which manifests itself in contention and discord between racial and ethnic groups; and it allures the carnal soul by encouraging lusts and satisfying desires and whims. It was clear, he said, that a civilization built on such principles could not bring the realization of harmonious life to humanity. The attainment of such a life would be far from people with a mentality based on such principles, which turn the world into a hell.

On the other hand, Islamic civilization is based on truth, instead of force. It states that "Might does not make right." Instead of self-interest, its aims are virtue and love. Instead of racialism and nationalism, it sees the bonds between masses as unity of religion, country, and class. Life is viewed not as a competition, but as cooperation. In place of lust and passion, its form of service is guidance and the essential characteristic of guidance is progress and prosperity in a way that is befitting to humanity, as well as enlightenment and perfection in a way that is required by the spirit. Therefore, Islamic civilization will correct the wrong assumptions underpinning the present-day civilization, and provide for the future happiness of humankind.

Bediüzzaman finishes the description of his vision as follows:

> As one, the council showed their assent to the predictions. They said, "Do not lose hope! The loudest and strongest voice in the coming upheavals and changes will be the voice of Islam."

QUESTIONS

1) To be at the service of which of the following is the highest level a servant could reach?

   A) the Qur'an   C) country

   B) family   D) global organization

2) Who is the author of the book, *Anadolu Efsaneleri* (Anatolian Tales)?

   A) Ömer Seyfettin   C) M. Necati Sepetçioğlu

   B) Tarık Buğra   D) Yavuz Bahadıroğlu

3) Which of the following terms best describes the state of "dignified contentment"?

   A) *Ikhlas*   C) *Sadaqat*

   B) *Istighna*   D) *Qadar*

4) "I can live without bread, I cannot live without _____!"
In the quote from Bediüzzaman above, which best fills the blank?

   A) water   C) freedom

   B) country   D) family

5) Who said the following sentence: "Brothers, I have come to Ankara for a personal matter. Therefore, I could not stay with you. If I had come for *hizmet*, service to faith, then I would stay with you."?

   A) Zübeyir   C) Bayram

   B) Hulusi   D) Sungur

6) Bediüzzaman wanted to draw the attention of the Sultan, the scholars, and the community of educational institutions. For that reason, where did he gather the scholars and the students, the politicians and the soldiers to do scholarly debates?

   A) Şekerci Han   C) Sultanahmet Mosque

   B) Topkapı Palace   D) Dolmabahçe Palace

7) Who is the scholar who hung a signboard which read, "If any-one, religious or irreligious, philosopher or scholar, from school or madrasa, has a question regarding any kind of knowledge or sci-ences, he may ask me. From you the question, from me the answer... but I shall not question anyone."

   A) Mawlana Jalaluddin Rumi

   B) Ibn Sina

   C) Al-Farabi

   D) Bediüzzaman Said Nursi

8) Who is one of the brothers of Bediüzzaman?

   A) Zübeyir   C) Bayram Yüksel

   B) Abdülmecid   D) Mustafa Sungur

9) Bediüzzaman says, "You should know that all your power lies in _____. Which one of the following best fills in the blanks?

   A) ethics   C) sincerity and truth

   B) philosophy   D) business

CHAPTER 5

THE QUR'AN

What Is the Purpose of the Qur'an Being Revealed to Us?

Before everything else, it was revealed so that the Qur'an itself would be understood. When the Qur'an is understood, we have happiness and tranquility in this world and the next. Its words are not magical sayings. A person who understands the Qur'an would establish a personal relationship with the Creator easily, and would become happy and peaceful.

The Qur'an explains that no matter what state a human is in, he should ask the All-Compassionate for forgiveness, and never lose hope. The necessity of establishing interpersonal relationships on the foundations of love, respect, brotherhood, justice, and tolerance is understood best through the Qur'an.

When we have understood the Quran, we see that it explains what is good and bad, and exposes benefits and consequences. While encouraging one, it discourages the other, it brings out examples of behavior that is praised and abhorred. "*Assuredly, We have struck for humankind in this Qur'an all kinds of parables and comparisons, so that they may reflect and be mindful*" (az-Zumar 39:27).

For that reason, first we turn to the life of the noble Messenger, from whom we extract the perfect example, then we resort to the lives of the Companions, and finally, to human intelligence and reasoning. Peering through the threads of the Book (the Holy Qur'an) and the Sunnah, we ponder the woven field of *ra'y* (considered opinion). However, by all means, the language of the Qur'an should be exposed and the works in the Islamic world must be reviewed by all means.

The Qur'an was revealed for human beings, who were taught how to use it during Prayer by our dear Prophet. But today, our people do not know the Qur'an as it should be known. They don't even try to know. They know only as much as they could need to read during the Prayer. But in reality, while one reads the Qur'an, one must internalize it; the one who reads should think, contemplate, and try to feel the breezes blowing from within it.

Otherwise, we have not understood it. The Qur'an should be taken as a whole, handled in its entirety. In order to fully understand the Qur'an, one must know something from the Sunnah, the behavior of our dear Prophet.

The Sunnah is the expression of the Qur'an in everyday life. If the Sunnah is not known, the Qur'an cannot be fully understood. The author of the Turkish national anthem, Mehmet Akif Ersoy, wrote the following lines about the Qur'an:

Although we recite it from memory every day, we do not derive a lesson from it!

Is it reasonable not to seek a purpose in these verses?

We see then that only its words are important;

Because we are not interested in its meaning,

Either we open up a page and stare;

Or we read and exhale while passing by a cemetery!

Benefitting from the Qur'an depends on complete concentration. For this marvelous, perfect transmitter, one needs a receiver. It is necessary to share the same frequency. Among us, there might be memorizers of it. But if all the things we read and memorize do not awaken in us the thought of reviewing our lives, then we have not benefitted.

How Is the One Who Reads the Qur'an and the One Who Doesn't?

In a *hadith*, our noble Prophet explains as follows the situation of the one who recites the Qur'an:

> The believer who recites the Qur'an is like a citron whose fragrance is sweet and whose taste is delicious. The believer who does not recite the Qur'an is like a date-fruit which has no fragrance but has a sweet taste. The hypocrite who recites the Qur'an is like basil whose fragrance is so sweet, but its taste is bitter. The hypocrite who does not recite the Qur'an is like a colocynth which has no fragrance and its taste is bitter.

The outer and inner world of the believer who consistently reads the Qur'an are enlightened. With its scent he spreads to humanity peace and tranquility.

Angels, Mercy and Tranquility Descends Where the Qur'an Is Recited

Reading and listening to the recitation of the Qur'an is a form of worship. So exalted a book is the Qur'an that not only human beings, but angels too enjoy a share of its recitation. They come to a place where the Qur'an is recited and enable the blowing of a Divine atmosphere therein. The Messenger of Allah expresses this reality with the following words: "Any group of people that assemble in one of the Houses of Allah to study the Qur'an, tranquility will descend upon them, mercy will engulf them, angels will surround them and Allah will make mention of them to those (the angels) in His proximity."

Usayd bin Khudayr, one of the Companions of the noble Prophet narrated:

One night, while I was harvesting dates, I was reciting al-B-aqarah, (the second chapter from the Qur'an). My horse was tied close by and it rose up on its back feet. Upon my horse's reaction to the recitation of this verse, I stopped and the horse calmed down. After a while, I began to recite it again, which made the horse rise on its feet again. My son, Yahya, was standing closer to the horse than I was. I meant to move my son to a safe distance from the horse in order to protect him. So, I walked up to my son. Suddenly, I raised my head up to the sky for a second only to be surprised at what I saw. There hovered something that was similar to an umbrella in the sky and there were objects inside the umbrella that resembled lanterns. I told what I saw in the field to the Messenger of Allah in the morning and he asked me: "Do you know what those things were?"

Hearing that I had no idea about the things that I saw, he explained: "They were the angels. Your voice invited them. If you had continued until morning, they would have continued to listen to you. And everyone would have seen them since they would not have hidden from the people."

The Important Duty

God, the Exalted One, sent His Messenger the verses of the Qur'an via Jibril, one of the archangels. Gabriel read the verses of the Qur'an to the Messenger of Allah, and he had his scribes write them down. Many of the Companions learned these verses by heart. The vast majority of Companions preferred learning the verses by heart because they knew very well the utmost importance of this practice. It was also because in those times, written language was not well-developed, and they believed in the power of their memory. Thus, the number of those that memorized the Qur'an increased.

Anyone powerful enough used to join the battles in those times. Those memorized the Qur'an were also among the names that died in the battles. Umar realized this situation, and he began to worry that the probability that the number of people memorizing the Qur'an would decrease. He sought solutions to prevent this. He decided to discuss one of his solutions with Abu Bakr.

One day while they were talking about the problems of the Muslims, he explained his thoughts in this way:

"In the Battle of Yamama, more than seventy people who memorized the whole Qur'an died. I fear that in the upcoming battles more people knowing Qur'an by heart will die. If this happens, the Qur'an will be incomplete. Therefore, we need to take some precautions right now. We shall collect the words of God and make them written.

Abu Bakr understood Umar's concern very well. However, he had a different concern as well. He said to Umar:

"How can I dare do something that the Messenger of Allah did not do?"

Since it was a big problem, Umar insisted on his opinion and said:

"My brother, I swear by God that this is a very propitious work."

Later he added the underlying reasons for his views in a detailed way. Thus, Umar persuaded Abu Bakr.

Upon this, Abu Bakr immediately called Zayd ibn Thabit to talk. Zayd was one of the scribes of God's Messenger. Abu Bakr explained to Zayd the concerns of Umar and his solution alike. Having listened to all of this, Zayd addressed Umar in this way:

"O Umar! How can we do something that the Messenger of Allah had never done before?"

Umar was about to answer this question, but Abu Bakr started to speak:

"I asked Umar the same question. Yet alone these words of his satisfied me. When the Messenger of Allah was alive, such a situation would not have occurred. If such a thing had happened, God would have sent the whole Qur'an again to the Messenger of Allah through revelation. Yet, now it is not possible for such a thing to come into being. That's why we need to take precaution."

Zayd had never thought about this before, and he found Umar's approach to be the right one. This important mission, upon the insistence of Umar, was given to Zayd by Abu Bakr. Zayd, after a series of long efforts to this end, achieved this mission. He meticulously collected the verses of the Qur'an that had been scattered so far. He collected all of them in the form of the Qur'an and handed it to the caliph. Thus, it was Zayd who was granted with the honor of collecting the verses of the Qur'an in written form.

Why Must We Love Our Nation?

Fethullah Gülen explains the reason why we must love our nation in the following way:

"Let me state, first of all, that I love my nation with respect to its collective spiritual personality. Otherwise, there can of course be individuals, among our nation as with every other, who can be considered deplorable from the perspective of truth, justice, and humanity. However, when taking into consideration our nation, which is generally firmly connected to their spiritual roots, it is evident that such individuals have remained a minority."

In a saying often related as a Prophetic Tradition, it is said: "Love of the homeland comes from belief." This can also be expressed as, "Love of nation is a part of faith." For our exalted nation who has been the standard-bearer of our religion of Islam for centuries has frequently changed the course of the history of humanity, and has served humanity in a great many ways. It is by virtue of this that we love our nation with a sense of pride.

Without question, our nation has accomplished great feats. These "accomplishments," generally call to mind, in our day, positive and technological advancements. However, knowledge and technology itself are not everything when it comes to solving the problems of humanity and securing its happiness and peace. Moreover, that scientific discoveries and technological progress bereft of morality, virtue, and a consciousness of social responsibility each become a scourge and disaster in the hands of the selfish and self-interested, is an incontrovertible reality. Consequently, implied in our statement, "Our nation has accomplished great feats," is the human and moral values our predecessors brought to all humanity and its dispersing justice to its surrounds by virtue of that exceptional capacity of administration and politics. We take an interest in these aspects of our nation and even have an attachment to it to the degree of love.

However, I cannot know whether all these affections will avail those people who are now in the past. Perhaps recalling these favors will be a means to remembering them in kindness. We can say, "May God have mercy on our forefathers! They left for us a promising country; however, we have polluted its countenance and what falls upon us now is to re-illuminate its horizon once again," and perhaps then this would mean something. Ultimately, if we claim to take a keen interest in, have an attachment and even a great love for our nation, which has developed upon firm spiritual roots, then we must fulfill those duties towards that beloved that are incumbent upon us. The issue of real importance for us is precisely this.

EDUCATIONAL ASPECT
OF FETHULLAH GÜLEN

Fethullah Gülen as an Educator

All the activities of Fethullah Gülen can be considered within the concept of education. According to him, all the problems we encounter on earth lie within humanity. That is to say, all problems start with the human and end with the human. Whether it is an organization that runs with little efficiency or none at all, or an unjust social system, or troubles to take place on the other side of the grave, the most effective solution is education. Therefore, education is tantamount, and teaching is the most sacred of vocations. The best and most beneficial service to a country and a nation can be carried out through education. (Hulusi Turgut, "Fethullah Gülen ve Okullar" (Fethullah Gülen and the Schools)", *Yeni Yüzyıl*, 15 January 1998).

The Educational Vision of Fethullah Gülen

According to Gülen, man can attain true life only by acquiring science, knowledge and insight. For this reason, those who are negligent in learning and teaching are deemed dead although they are physically alive. Man is created to observe, know and convey what he learns to other people. A person acts more properly and gives more felicitous decisions to the extent he is more closely engaged in reason and logic, which are illuminated and perfected only through science and knowledge. For this reason, without science and knowledge, reason would be stagnant and logic would be deceitful and decisions would be erring. True quality of humanness of a person is manifested by the process of this person's learning, teaching and illuminating others. A person who is ignorant in many respects, but does not consider learning about them and refrains from renovating himself and setting a good example for others can be safely questioned about his human qualities. Positions or ranks acquired thanks to science and knowledge are superior than and outlive those obtained via other methods. Indeed, knowledge makes its owner not only virtuous and away from evil and harm in this world, but also happy and delighted with stations he acquires through it in the Hereafter. Hearts that are devoid of truth and souls that are destitute of knowledge will, on the other hand, serve nothing but as a hotbed for all sorts of evil ideas. (*Ölçü veya Yoldaki Işıklar*, 22).

Education and training are two lofty tasks coming from the heavens. These tasks are nothing but manifestation in human life of the God's Attribute of Sustainer, and with the fulfillment of this task, merits and qualifications of human soul are brought to surface and readied for being presented to the society as a gift. As a person that has not gone through distilling mechanisms of education and training fail to develop human virtues and elevating traits, he will certainly lack social qualities as well. (*Sızıntı*, 10 November 1979).

For him, education or training is a vital issue that must be accentuated not only by individuals, but also by societies. First of all, an individual is a human being to the extent his feelings are far away or free from foul things. Whether those people with hearts that are under the pressure of evil thoughts and with souls that are torturing in the cauldron of carnal desires can be considered as proper human beings is dubious. Those qualities of upbringing and training that relate to physical qualities may be perceptible to everyone, but I presume there are few people who truly comprehend the significance of the intellectual, emotional and spiritual education that promotes one to the state of being a true human being. Second, amelioration of a nation can be best served not by destroying what is evil, but by elevating the generations to humanity within the context of a program of education and upbringing based on universal facts and national values. Without sowing the holy seeds that are but a mixture of beliefs, ideals, historical awareness, dedication for servicing the nation and humankind and traditions to every parcel of land across the country, you will find a new evil popping up to replace the one you just destroyed. (*Ölçü veya Yoldaki Işıklar*, 150).

Nations can survive only thanks to new generations. Any nation that seeks to secure its future must, in addition to investing time and energy to various tasks, allocate part of its resources to education and training of children and young people who will become adults in future. This is because a child to continuation of human kind and species is what a seed or kernel is to continuation of the tree kind and species. Nations that neglect their children are doomed to collapse and those that entrust them to completely foreign and vulgar people are destined to lose their essence and spirit. The generations that form the most active and efficient part of a nation for every 30 or 40 years are yesterday's children. The people in charge 30 or 40 years are to be blamed for evil qualities that we observe in current generations as well as much criticized unwanted characteristics of administrators such as incompetence, ineptitude and incapacity and for the problems troubling the nation.

All sorts of evil qualities or virtues that will emerge after a quarter of a century will be blamed on those who assume the education and upbringing of today's generations. Thus, those who want to make prophecies about the future of a nation should look at the current upbringing provided to children and young people of that nation and in this way will they certainly be able to make accurate and unerring predictions. For this reason, while investments in other areas may prove wasteful to a large extent, anything done for the sake of promoting generations to the level of true humanity will remain as a never-ending source of wealth and income. (*Ölçü veya Yoldaki Işıklar*, 142–143).

According to him, there is a close relation between the social structures of nations and their educational principles. A society is gradually shaped according to education and training provided to its members. Indeed, the generations who are being trained and educated today will take office as the trainers of tomorrow and give what they learned from their instructors to their students. Education is as vital for moral and social lives of nations as marriage and reproduction for continuation of their bodily existence. As the nations which have failed to introduce sound and well-established rules and principles to their marital affairs will be doomed to destruction, those who do not attach due importance to the spiritual and moral condition of the society will not be able to survive for a long time.

QUESTIONS

1) "Although we recite it from memory every day, we do not derive a lesson from it!

Is it reasonable not to seek a purpose in these verses?

We see then that only its words are important;

Because we are not interested in its meaning,

Either we open up a page and stare;

Or we read and exhale while passing by a cemetery!"

The above lines were written by which author?

A) Mehmet Akif Ersoy   C) Necip Fazıl Kısakürek

B) Arif Nihat Asya   D) Yahya Kemal Beyatlı

2) "The believer who recites the Qur'an is like a _____ whose fragrance is sweet and whose taste is delicious. Which best fills in the blank?

A) orange   C) citron

B) grapefruit   D) tangerine

3) "The hypocrite who recites the Qur'an is like _____ whose fragrance is so sweet, but its taste is bitter." Which best fills in the blank?

A) oleander   C) basil

B) hashish   D) date palm

4) Which of the following does not come down to a place where the Qur'an is recited?

A) angels   C) tranquility

B) mercy   D) heedlessness

5) The All-Glorified sent the Qur'anic verses to our noble Prophet through which angel?

A) Azrail   C) Israfil

B) Mikail   D) Jibril

6) Which Companion recorded the revelation to the Messenger of Allah, and collected the first written form of the Qur'an?

A) Zayd

B) Bilal

C) Abu Bakr

D) Umar

7) Whose opinion regarding the love of one's country is discussed in the article "Why Must We Love Our Nation?"

A) Mehmet Akif Ersoy

B) Fethullah Gülen

C) Necip Fazıl Kısakürek

D) Bediüzzaman Said Nursi

8) _____ and _____ are two lofty tasks coming from the heavens. Which words best fill in the blanks?

A) Education, technology

B) Education, training

C) Manners, technology

D) Manners, technology

9) The nations neglecting their children are doomed to fall, and those who leave them to untrained hands are doomed to lose their essence. Every _____ years, the new generation, yesterday's children, are the most fruitful and active part of a nation. Which numbers best fill in the blank?

A) 30–40

B) 20–30

C) 40–50

D) 50–60

CHAPTER 6

FETHULLAH GÜLEN: AN ISLAMIC SCHOLAR, PREACHER AND PHILANTHROPIST

Gülen and Private Schools

The private high schools established upon Fethullah Gülen's encouragement became important in two respects: first, in terms of their social aspect; and second, in terms of the quality of education.

They greatly enhanced interest in education everywhere, in circles that supported or criticized them. In a sense, these colleges contributed to spreading education to non-governmental organizations and made education the possession of larger segments of society. As the success stories realized by these schools started to receive broad coverage and public attention, people were compelled to show great interest in educational projects. Turkey was new to such an emphasis on education, having never experienced such an event in its history. Today, special education programs in the media, and special features on the news, which regard education have become ordinary practice. Now, many people from all kinds of ideological backgrounds, professionals or amateurs in this field, open colleges in an organized manner. Education is a growing field in the private sector that gains importance with each passing day. And it has been the schools attributed to the Gülen Movement and their successes that have triggered these developments.

In addition to all of this, these schools have ushered in a notion of selfless service to education. Education is a long-lasting marathon. It requires serious effort and hard work. The success of these schools is based on altruism and idealism. Thousands of people serve in these institutions with unabated enthusiasm. They act with a sense of contentment, and they illustrate the idea of a soul dedicated to humanity.

This is the attitude that the Turkish education system forgot long ago. Of course, there are altruistic and faithful people everywhere. However, it has been nearly impossible to attract teachers to regions of deprivation. In some regions, the application of double salaries has been established as an economic incentive. Despite such a generous offer, teachers prefer to work in big cities where modern consumption habits are more easily satisfied. Since teachers who want to work for public schools start their career in a district selected by the Ministry of Education according to priorities, the issue of appointments and placements has been the most complicated, controversial and speculative agenda for Turkey. But there is no such a problem in schools associated with Gülen. A harmonious framework of employment and teaching environment is what signifies these schools. The teachers go to the most remote corners of the world, some that are plagued by deprivation. Among these are regions where military conflict with separatist groups is an ongoing reality. Despite these facts, however, the teachers appointed to these dangerous regions head there with an utter sense of acceptance and assurance of their future. "They would like to show, acting for this cause, that education is serious and it requires sacrifice and altruism, submission, and resignation." There is no doubt that the architect of this devotion to humanity and a sound understanding of trusting in God (*tawakkul*) is Fethullah Gülen. But what has drawn a man who comes from the madrasa system into the field of modern education? Why would someone who is aging and has had a difficult medical history engage in such a marathon? Some people ask similar questions from a reverse angle: What does a religious person have to do with education? If he is a preacher or *hodja* (religious teacher), why does not he keep himself confined to his own specialization? These have been the questions asked by media groups and by various people from different sectors of society. These questions were answered in interviews held on various occasions, according to the context in which the questions were raised.

Gülen is almost the only person who has, both directly and indirectly, paid so much attention to the issue of education. In his sermons, conversations, articles, and essays, he has struggled to present the need to engage the masses in educational projects. He has tried to relay his message to all sectors of society, but especially to tradesmen and artisans who have come to listen to his sermons and lectures; he has exhorted them strongly to deal with the lack of proper education in the society.

In the near history of the Republic, the issue of education has been normally restricted to a handful of ideologues and politicians. Education has been a field over which only an enlightened group of people pondered, talked, debated and put forward projects. The large masses of society have not been permitted to participate in these discussions in any way. The matter of education has been regarded too important to entrust to the general public! That has been the general attitude of Turkish intellectuals. They could never think that a large community of tradesmen would mobilize their economic capacity for education without expecting any profit. As a matter of fact, the grassroots had never assumed any role in such political, educational, or socio-cultural projects. Fethullah Gülen challenged this perspective, and the elite character of its proponents.

He argued that such a perspective alienates people from education, politics, and the state.

Gülen regards and defines the matter of education as the biggest problem of not only our country but also of contemporary modern civilization. He believes that the education of humankind is the foundation of faith. At the root of the modern education crisis lies the fragmentation of the once-harmonious heart and mind connection in education and scientific thinking. Gülen contends that the new education system will not be able quell this crisis unless it redefines the natural and inherent relationship between humanity, the cosmos, and God. For the last couple of centuries, modern scientific thought and education has turned all humane, social, and ideological relationships into profane objects, stripping them of their sacredness and ascribing to them a positivist nature.

This situation has led to corruption and a spiritual crisis that society currently witnesses. One of the innovations developed by Gülen is his holistic outlook in regard to the relationship between human being, the cosmos, and God—namely the harmonious unity of mind and heart. The colleges inspired by his ideas have questioned and overcome this extremely positivistic problem that deadlocks contemporary thought and education systems. It goes without saying that these schools do not offer their students a religious education. However, they do treat mind and heart simultaneously as the center of information and thought, and offer a system that views humans as existing in a harmonious relationship with the universe, society, and God. These schools work to create model individuals who are confident in themselves and the future; who are at peace with their own personality; who are respectful of their traditions, the roots of their faith, and their social identity; and who are open to modern scientific thought, innovation, and change. That is why, everywhere they have been opened, these colleges represent a new voice in education, and an excellent model of successful, hard-working, and open-minded students.

In addition, these colleges have changed the clumsy understanding of education as it was defined by blind repetition, which was based on memorization of definite patterns. The Turkish education system is still mostly dependent on memorization. It is under the yoke of formal logic in many fields. The educational program at these schools established a mathematical and experimental form of logic, and a progressive method that is not based on memorization or repetition.

They have brought a new dynamism to education. They have transformed the formerly stagnant and lazy attitude of Turkish education, improving and highlighting student learning in all subjects.

Another significant development emerging from these schools is in the realm of student-teacher, school-parent, and student-student relationships. The colleges promote an emotional, sincere, and heartfelt order of relations between all the people involved in a student's education. From this point of view, the colleges have reproduced genuine and positive relations between the family, street, and community, and they have adapted these relations to modern conditions. They reconstruct the former self-sacrificing "person of society," who is totally devoted to his or her nation and to humanity, and who is the hero of love and affection. In this era, when selfishness, egotism and materialism prevail, this is a remarkable achievement. In a time dominated by the primacy of material interests and idolization of personal, this new form of education is leading students to prefer the profession of teaching over all others.

While there are highly respected occupations in aviation, computer and industrial engineering, medicine, etc., which provide social status and prestige, these people choose teaching. These teachers take these merits with them wherever they go. Each of them thus becomes "an ambassador of culture." Many of the places they go are not even suitable for tourists; but despite material deprivation, these teachers meet their surroundings with high spirit.

They establish warm relations with local people in those countries, and thus form a historic bridge. It is difficult to gauge the impact this bridge will have on behalf of Turkey, but it is not difficult to predict that the schools will enable Turkey and the co-operating countries the possibility of establishing and improving broad relations on a humane and social basis. (Enes Ergene, *Tradition Witnessing the Modern Age*, 124–129).

INTELLECTUAL ASPECT OF FETHULLAH GÜLEN AND DIALOGUE

Why Dialogue?

Though interfaith dialogue activities constitute one of the foundational legs of the Gülen Movement (or the Hizmet Movement), dialogue definitely did not begin with him. In the 1960s, the Roman Catholic Church took a significant step toward dialogue with Jews and Muslims. Surely, this could not be tied only to one factor. As professor Suat Yıldırım said, there are many other factors involved. In order to maintain its existence, Church leaders felt it was necessary to open up and reach out to the rest of the world, and desired to restore the appeal it is increasingly losing; feeling a kinship to the Islam, which accepts Abraham as the patriarch of *tawhid* (the Oneness and Unity of God).

Because of the attacks on Islam throughout the ages, some Muslim circles have approached every effort made by the Church with utter cynicism. Because of these attacks and the doubts caused by them, they remained in a defensive mood. Due to these circumstances, and the events taking place outside their hands, they take a stand or change their stance and consider this as a defense of Islam. They quit taking initiative on behalf of Islam a long time ago. These circles, even more than those who shrink from the activities initiated by Gülen, actually strenuously object to the tolerance and dialogue activities of Hizmet Movement, along with the adherents of other religions.

Today, there is no healthy ground where Islam can be explained properly. The modern world is far ahead of the Muslims in matters of politics and economics that modern men give priority to. The superiority of the Muslims in such fields belongs to history.

What the Muslims must do today is bring to the fore what the modern world needs more than anything else: the universal values of Islam, its system of worship, its perspective of the universe and existence. They can end the centuries-old dispute between science and religion.

Introduction and representation of these principles requires an atmosphere of reconciliation, peace, and dialogue. In a climate of war and confrontation, nothing can be accomplished. Circles who passionately, vigorously, and consciously oppose dialogue activities would never want such an atmosphere to be established.

Irresponsible actions by individuals damage the image of Islam and destroy the very tradition they are claiming to defend. Unfortunately, the scenarios supporting the terrorist acts have blackened the image of Islam.

In the contemporary world, though it is not like that in practice, discussions abound on basic human rights and freedoms, democracy, free enterprise, love, tolerance, dialogues, and the importance attached to the individual. Though there would be some reservations, these are values Islam does not oppose.

The introduction of Islam, which represents these values in theory, creed, historical practice and jurisprudence, in totally opposite terms turns the message upside down. In a world established on the foundations of dispute, confrontation and fighting, the Muslims do not have power to prove the opposite. Therefore, presenting Islam with its true essence and values that would attract modern people, is dependent on the existence of a milieu of peace, dialogue, tolerance, and reconciliation. We have this reality before us.

The West is far ahead of the Islamic world in economic, political and military matters. Belief, devotion, and manners remain vital, but in a world where materialistic factors and causes prevail, economic power is necessary.

In our day, through the intensification of communication and transportation, the world has become like a small village. Anything happening in one corner of the globe influences the rest; and all relationships have become interactive. In order for us to live together, it is necessary to create a milieu wherein everyone can live his own faith and be respectful of the faith of others. This, too, favors the Muslims.

Only now is it possible to find among important intellectuals, Christian clergy, and men of religion a softening in the attitude towards Islam, and even a closeness to it. Other than Karen Armstrong, the author of the very important book, *Muhammad: A Biography of the Prophet*, Massingnon, Charles J. Ledit, Y. Moubarac, Irene M. Dalmais, L. Gardet, Norman Daniel, Michel Leliong, H. Maurier, Olivier Lacombe, Thomas Merton, Sidney Griffith, Thomas Mitchell, John Esposito and Dale F. Eickelman can be counted, along with some clergy and others.

With their genuine, warm feelings toward Islam and our noble Prophet, they are also sincere proponents of dialogue between followers of different religions. The continuation of this atmosphere is crucial for our world, humanity, and of course, Muslims. This requires a warm atmosphere of dialogue, tolerance, and peace.

As a prominent thinker of ours stated, our world is sliding into an age of knowledge, and to a great extent, knowledge will rule. A Muslim who does not doubt Islam, who knows that Islam proves its principles through science, sees dialogue with the adherents of other religions as important, not a thing that makes no difference. For a Muslim who is conscious of his function, meaning, and duties in the world, it is *sine qua non*, it is essential.

For many years the Muslim subconscious has been anxious, living in fear that outsiders will snatch them away. They remained in a defensive posture, believing that they were surrounded by enemies; a belief so strong and pervasive it was, as it were, the sixth pillar of Islam. It is long overdue to burst out of their self-imposed prison, and become aware of the outside world.

For too long the world has been a place of progress for others, and a place of backwardness for us. Why should this continue? Why should Islam be the religion of desolation, ruin, heedlessness, and frozen hearts? Why should Muslims be insulted and humiliated while earning their livelihood in other countries, marginalized in the new world, lost to themselves and disdained by others? In order to overcome all this, there is but one requirement.

The Muslims cannot use Islam as a vehicle for their ego, as a way of being superior to others for their adherence, as a stepping stone for their worldly ambitions. This image has never belonged to Islam, and it cannot be. Let Muslims discover their faith, before anything else, as a religion, and then let them represent it as such. First and foremost, we change the image of Islam in their minds.

Gülen's Journey to the United States

Starting in June 1999 with a Turkish channel, various cassette recordings were broadcast, one after another. The conversations, which contained no criminal elements, were spliced together to provoke a wave of indignation and outrage among the public.

During this storm staged against Fethullah Gülen, the much -discussed virtues of democracy and a free press—like fairness and human rights—were completely forgotten during the bombardment, which continued for many days.

During the case initiated by the broadcast of the cassettes, Fethullah Gülen was found not guilty. The trial made it clear that the cassettes were disseminated to slander him, and to blacken the Hizmet Movement. To be clear, only two cases were ever initiated against Gülen, and only in one was he convicted, under martial law, to the now-lifted Article 163.

Nearly a year later, the prosecutor of the Ankara National Security Court issued an arrest warrant. The August 3 request was rejected four days later because "no evidence of the crime was present." The prosecutor repeated his request on August 11 and an arrest warrant was issued. Gülen's lawyers disputed the charge, and the Istanbul prosecutor cancelled the warrant. But on October 16, the case went ahead.

That same year, the Turkish Writers Association gave a Superior Service Award to Fethullah Gülen. But the case against him continued through 2002 and 2003. While responding to the trumped-up charges against him, he continued to make strides for world peace, and deal with failing health.

His body, disturbed at different stages by all manner of illness, is very sensitive. On March 31, 2002, he was taken to an emergency room due to chronic heart failure and diabetes. He was discharged on April 2 after treatment.

In 2004, he gave two lengthy interviews. The first interview, given to Nuriye Akman, was printed in *Zaman*, a Turkish daily, on March 22, 2004. It was also published in book format later. The second interview, given to Mehmet Gündem, was published as a series in January 2005 in *Milliyet*, another daily. It was also later published in book format. That same year, he gave interviews to various members of domestic and foreign press.

He went to America in 1999 for medical treatment. Under his doctors' advice, he continues living in a retreat house belonging to Golden Generation Foundation in Pennsylvania. Due to his health problems, he remains there. His love for Turkey, because of his absence and longing, finds echo in every word, every poem, such as "Hüzünlü Gurbet" (Sorrowful Separation).

He is homesick for Turkey. In America, where is he is obligated to remain due to the nature of his illness, which sometimes prevents him even from standing. In his poetry, prose, and interviews, his longing for his country is clear.

Gülen's homesickness has meant even refusing to launder the garments he last wore while departing Turkey. When a guest asked him about the clothes, he replied, "Yes, since I came here, I protect them. I have never let them be washed. I did not even allow the dust to be wiped away. In the dust is Turkey."

In his room he keeps soil brought from the four corners of Turkey. The room where he stays is like a confidant, a witness to all his suffering. Whenever a negative event takes place anywhere in the world he feels the sadness through every inch of his soul, and sometimes visits the rooms adjacent to the corridor, in order to find a friend for his heart.

Fethullah Gülen does not allow a conversation to take pace if it is not useful for issues in this world or the next. In his speeches, he brings the subject around to Allah and His Messenger. He has no use for empty talk. His doctors advise Gülen, who practice his religion in a fastidious way, not to fast during Ramadan due to the nature of his diabetes, but he continues to anyway. "I would tell the people who are in my condition not to fast, but I cannot tell it to myself," he said. Fasting renders him immobile because of his ailment, but as he never neglects any of his devotions, he cannot neglect the fast, either. Surely, to understand the life of Fethullah Gülen is to study the makeup of his character.

One Should Have Broad Knowledge in Religious Matters

A person, who is expected to communicate the message and represent his faith, should possess extensive knowledge about his own religion before he could explain it to others. Otherwise, grave mistakes can be made in the name of religion and those who are doing the invitation can frighten people away from religion and themselves. Initially, one should have comprehensive knowledge on the Qur'an, the Book of God. Along with the text of the Qur'an, one should also learn about its meaning and spirit. In this regard, one should refer to the interpretation and exegesis of the Qur'an. In addition to this, the life of our noble Prophet and the lives of his Companions should be studied through *hadith* narrations and history of Islam. Finally, one should study *ilmihal* (the basics of the Islamic faith) and books that will help him gather the necessary information which he aims to convey to others.

In relation to Islamic knowledge, we have two main sources: the Qur'an and the Sunnah. When explaining religion to others, one should remain within the principles of these two sources and possess comprehensive knowledge about them. We should digest the topics that we will explain to others, so well that the people we address could also be nourished with ease.

As Bediüzzaman stated, we should be like sheep when we feed others, not like birds which feed their young with spew. We should process what we learned and convert it into milk and let it flow into the needy hearts like some water of life, a fountain of remedy. Through such method, this information will enter their hearts and produce a honey comb and honey in the name of wisdom and knowledge.

Of course, this could only occur through reading and understanding and also through the expansion of our culture and knowledge. For this reason, those who have taken on the duty of invitation to the universal virtues must reserve a certain part of their day to reading. A person who is deprived of the culture of his era will have nothing to offer to today's society. In other words, a person who has insufficient knowledge about culture will not be able to satisfy the person addressed for too long. Consequently, a person who is in contact with people of all levels must possess enough knowledge to satisfy his audience.

Indeed, those who have made *irshad* (invitation and guidance to virtues) an objective of their lives must be well equipped with the necessary knowledge. The words of an empty person will also be empty. Moreover, such people who have nothing to offer will try to cover up their ignorance with rage and violence. In reaction to such conduct, people they address will refuse to accept even the most logical and simple issues.

Owning up to Religion Is a Primary Obligation upon All Believers

In this day and age, supporting religion which means spreading its message is a primary obligation for all believers. No believer is excluded from this imperative duty. Indeed, all believers must learn their religion and put it into practice in their daily lives. And then, they should explain their experiences to others so that the world of others could also be illuminated with Divine light.

In all periods of history there have been people who are in need of guidance. Believers traveling on the same boat with those who are wasting their lives in the valleys of misguidance thus looking for a way out, are obligated to fulfill their responsibilities towards their co-travelers. This duty is a prerequisite of being human. Depending on their status, level and means available, everyone has an obligation towards this duty. Otherwise, being accountable for this duty on the Day of Judgment will be a difficult task.

When we scrutinize the history, we will see that those who have undertaken this noble duty of invitation and guidance have always followed the same path. After receiving this noble duty, the Messenger of Allah spent every day of his life conveying the message of religion. He would travel door to door looking for a friendly face and a heart to convey his message.

Initially, no one showed any consideration or interest. Later, some began to ridicule him. Gradually, their attitudes turned to harassment, insult, and torture. They were laying thorns on his path and pouring the internal organs of dead animals down his head as he stood for the Prayer. They believed that it was right to torture and harass the Messenger of Allah in all forms of manner. However, contrary to all attacks, the noble Messenger did not give an inch and never felt wearisome of his duty, because this was the very reason for his existence. He visited everyone repeatedly, including his archenemies. He conveyed the Divine message. Who knows how many times he visited Abu Jahl and Abu Lahab, archenemies of faith, and delivered the message of Islam to them! He was walking around the fairs and visiting all the tents with an intention to save the faith of one person. Wherever he went, doors would be shut on his face yet he would go again and again with the same message.

As Mecca became an unlivable place for the noble Messenger, he migrated to Medina. He was to spread his Divine light in this city then. He did not stay away from his duty of invitation and guidance, not even for a moment. He explained religion to the smallest detail and invited people to it. Throughout his stay in Medina, even during the conflicts, he did not withdraw from conveying his message to every individual.

Our noble Messenger was a unique individual who carried the weighty obligation of Prophethood on his shoulders for twenty-three years, fulfilling his responsibilities like no other man of action.

QUESTIONS

1) The cassette lynching launched against Fethullah Gülen and his sympathizers began in which year?

   A) 1999   C) 2001

   B) 2000   D) 2002

2) To which writer did Fethullah Gülen give a long interview in 2004?

   A) Nuh Gönültaş   C) Fehmi Koru

   B) Nuriye Akman   D) Ekrem Dumanlı

3) In which year did Fethullah Gülen settle in the United States?

   A) 1999   C) 2001

   B) 2000   D) 2002

4) Along with the text of the Qur'an, one should also learn about its _____. Which best fills in the blank?

   A) structure   C) meaning and spirit

   B) format   D) arrangement

5) To learn our religion we have in our hands two sources. Which of the following are these sources?

A) the Qur'an and the Universe

B) the Qur'an and the Sunnah

C) the Universe and the Sunnah

D) the Universe and the Holy Books

6) Who said: "We should be like sheep when we feed others, not like birds which feed their young with spew."

A) Fethullah Gülen

B) Mehmet Akif Ersoy

C) Bediüzzaman Said Nursi

D) Necip Fazıl Kısakürek

7) "Owning up to _____ is a primary obligation upon all believers." Which best fills in the blank?

A) country   C) family

B) nation   D) religion

8) Although his diabetes is serious and he has been advised not to, what kind of worship does Fethullah Gülen not forgo?

A) *Salah*   C) fasting

B) Hajj   D) supplications

CHAPTER 7

REPRESENTATION

Universal Language: The Language of Conduct

Traveling to other nations in order to spread the Divine message provides an important opportunity to learn new languages. Every Prophet conveyed his message through the tongue of his people. However, the success of the disciples cannot be based solely on the fact that they learned the language of the people who they invited to religion. I like to base this argument on a very significant historical event. Indeed, disciples have been quite effective in their representation in foreign lands. Their success lies in a universal language which they spoke. This language was the language of conduct and good manners. From the noble Messenger of Allah to his Companions and from the Companions to this day, the sultans of hearts have conquered many hearts and souls using this very language.

How the Companions learn the language of the people so rapidly in foreign lands is not that important. It might be that God rewarded them with this ability in return for their enthusiasm to spread the message of Islam or perhaps it was the fruits of their dedication.

For example, a Companion of the Prophet would leave Medina and travel to Spain for a higher purpose. He did not know their language or culture. The only thing that kept him on his feet was his dedication to this great cause and the dynamics which continuously nourished him. Not knowing the language was a disadvantage but it was a situation where causes had stopped and the Divine help had arrived. In recognition of his weakness, he lived the truth and conveyed his message through actions and good conduct. As a result, many people in the region came running towards the warm atmosphere of faith which he had formed.

When Mus'ab ibn Umayr left for Medina, he knew 12 verses from the Qur'an. Perhaps, the words he had spoken in Medina did not exceed five-hundred yet he was speaking with such a delicate language of manners that even the most stone-hearted people melted in his presence. Within a year, he came to Aqaba with seventy-two people.

It is also possible to show thousands of such examples in this day and age. For example, I like to share a story explained to me by some friends who enrolled in a language course following the September 11 tragedy. Muslims were treated differently after this tragic incident. It was a time when the media was portraying Muslims as people to be feared and this was the time that these friends had enrolled in the English classes. Because of their religion others were looking at them with spying eyes. Although they felt uncomfortable from these suspicious glances, they showed patience in the name of God and tried to explain themselves with their manners and behavior. The Holy Qur'an explains: "*Every one acts according to his own character*" (al-Isra 17:84). This means that everyone shows their character through their manner. As these particular friends displayed their characters through their manners, everyone got their share out of the atmosphere they had formed. They had earned the appraisal of everyone through the way they sat, walked, ate, spoke, behaved and displayed their gentleness. On the second day of the course, people apologized to them for the inappropriate behavior displayed by some students hence the good manners of these friends were appreciated.

Another incident they had experienced was: A foreign student who was in the same class stressed that he hated and despised Turks. As a reason he used an example from his country of origin, arguing that he had witnessed some incidents in which Turks had behaved in an unacceptable manner. They explained to him that these people do not represent the entire Turkish nation and that in every nation one would find good and evil people. A short while after, these friends purchased some imported foods from Turkey and shared them in the class. Gradually, they became the center of attention during the recess. Soon, the entire class began to develop a feeling of affection for these people.

One day, a student in the class invited them to a dinner in his house. Following the dinner, they offered their Prayers and interact with each other in a friendly atmosphere. As they left the house, their hosts made the following commentary: "Now we have four Turkish-Muslim brothers."

The tremors of September 11 and the negative approaches of the media had formed an unbearable atmosphere for the Muslims. However, these friends who had received a warm response from their classmates were encouraged from the positive developments. Their enthusiasm and eagerness had increased thus they evaluated the situation with the following remarks: "If every Muslim carried the attributes which they should possess, and applied them in their daily lives, there would be no obstacles they could not overcome in the name of these exalted ideals."

Let us conclude our topic with the words of a hero of role modeling: "If we could implement the values of faith in our lives within their real essence, then the followers of other religions will embrace this religion in masses." The existence of ideals and thoughts depends on its representatives. If the Companions of the noble Prophet had not lived the Qur'an as it should be lived, the Qur'an would have become a tongue-tied orphan. Looking at the issue from this perspective, if we do not want our values to turn into an orphan, then we need to take extreme care with our representation. Otherwise, we would pay dearly for our negligence. Therefore, one should not say: "How can I be a role model when I do not have much knowledge?" One should say: "It is more important to know a little but practice it through representation than to know a lot." Following this principle will provide a guarantee for us and the future generations.

How Does a White Man Serve an African?

We live in a poor suburb of Kenya. We have a simple life: A piece of dry bread we find is enough to make us happy for that day. My husband, children and I live in a small tin cabin. We never complain about our life. Many Kenyans live the way we do. We live in a narrow street and sewerage channels pass from the top of the dirt road that crosses our neighborhood. Death frequently visits our neighborhood. The scorching heat of the sun transforms our tin cabin into an oven. Malaria, dysentery and typhoid fever never leaves us alone.

There are also white men who live in our nation. We continue our lives without taking any notice of the space which exists between them and us. We have always been led to believe that white man is superior. They should be respected. Some people who come here to spread their religion always hinted that there is a difference between them and us. Although, they never mention it out in the open, they showed it with their actions and attitudes. They eat on different tables, they live in different houses and they ride on different vehicles.

We always dreamed of meeting white men who thinks like us. We hoped that the bad fortune of our Africa might change through such meeting. Yet, it never happened... Our story continued in this manner until the day we met these people. This was the day that my husband was employed by a Turkish school. Yes, these people were also white but their life-styles and manners had changed everything we believed about white people.

That summer, my husband Hasan started to work as a teacher in the Turkish school. I would never forget the words he uttered on the night of the day he had commenced his employment there: "Some of the administrative staff and teachers are white but these people are different to all the white men we know. We work under same conditions, we share the same food and on the same table. You may not believe this but they treat me and other Kenyans just as the way they treat their white friends. A white man brought us tea and he served it to all of us with a tray. The principal called me to his room and collected information about the living conditions in our neighborhood."

The things my husband explained were fascinating to me. How could a white man serve the Africans and share his food on the same table? These were behaviors that we had never seen before. I said to Hasan: "Maybe they are not sincere. They are new here and perhaps they need our support. A few months later they will begin to act like the other white people." However, months had gone by and their manners did not change, on the contrary, with each passing day, they came closer to us.

Each night when my husband came home, he would talk about them. I was looking for an opportunity to meet these people. I always carried a doubt in my head, as I thought to myself: "White man will never see himself as equal to us." The behavior of these people could be the policy of the school. One evening,

Hasan came home and with excitement in his eyes, he said: "Fatima, here is your chance to meet them. The principal wants to visit our home with a few guests from Turkey."

I was surprised because I thought such thing was not possible. Moreover, I was a bit upset with Hasan as I thought he was joking with me. I said to him: "Stop joking around with me." Hasan replied: "I am not joking, they are coming tomorrow evening."

My husband seemed quite serious. I knew him very well hence his tone of voice and facial expression indicated that he was not joking. I was a bit confused and this was evident on my face. I replied with a stern voice: "White men will never come to our house!" Suddenly, I began to weep. Why was I crying? Did these tears which I was shedding symbolize the Africa that I longed for so many years? Were these the light-faced people that we were waiting for? I could not wait for the next day. I had reservations: "Would they really come to our home?" What would they think of the conditions in which we live?

Then they came and one by one they hugged my husband. Then they greeted me with respect and kindly asked how I was. I was nervous as I felt like weeping with joy. These white men had greeted me like no one before with pure sincerity and genuineness. This was the first time I had seen an African and a white men hug each other with so much honesty. More importantly, they took my children into their arms, stroked their heads and kissed them. They looked quite happy in our tin cabin and showed no sign of discomfort. They had brought gifts to all of us. They sat with us for hours comfortably and with no hesitation.

This was the moment that I realized these people were the people with faces of light which we had been waiting for. Our tin cabin was witnessing a historical event. I believed that these were the people who would change the dark fate of our Africa.

NATIONAL CONSCIOUSNESS

The Sensitivity of Akif

Shortly before his death, a group of guests came to visit Mehmet Akif Ersoy. He was lying down, exhausted. The topic of conversation came around to the national anthem, and one of them said: "I wonder if it was written anew, would it not be nicer?" At once, Akif raised his head and said: "My brother, what are you saying? May our Creator not force this nation again to write another national anthem."

HISTORICAL
CONSCIOUSNESS

As Long as Such Mothers Are Alive!

It was freezing cold. The Ottomans wanted to prevent a land war, and guarded the straits of Çanakkale by concentrating the troops there. The 33rd regiment was being transferred to Çanakkale via Havran, Edremit, and Ezine, and the regiment settled in Havran that night. When a group of officers were meeting with the local villagers, an officer started to explain the status of preparations: "Muhtar (the elected village head) Effendi, you know how the weather is. In this cold weather if the soldiers are left outside, they will perish before reaching the front. And you could more or less estimate the number of the soldiers, too."

Muhtar seemed sure of himself. To the commander, he responded with a smile: "Be comfortable, Commander. We have already heard and made our preparations. The war does not take place only on the front lines. We, too, are a part of this war. Exactly what is your number?"

"Three thousand."

"How many beasts do you have?"

"About a hundred and fifty."

"How about your officers?"

"About fifty."

"Okay. We had estimated almost the same thing, Commander. Forty sheep were slaughtered and five pots of rice are cooked. For the animals, we have vacated four barns. The places for the officers and the troops are ready, too. We have assigned each house a suitable number. Commander, do you have any other wish?"

The commander felt a lump in his throat. "What else could we need, Muhtar? I want to thank you on behalf of my soldiers."

Units were sent to their assigned houses, one by one. Guards were assigned to certain places. The soldiers were fed and quartered. After some time, Lieutenant Şükrü walked around in the village square to see whether anyone needed an assignment. He came across an elderly woman who was walking with difficulty, using a walking stick. He ran to her aid, asking, "Grandma, what is going on? What are you looking for at this late hour of the night?"

She straightened up with the support of her staff. She directed her flashlight toward the officer's face. "I am looking for my children," she said.

"What? Did you lose your children?"

"O my son! Nine soldiers were supposed to come to me. Muhtar had told me so. I have prepared their places. I have waited a long time, and no one showed up. I got curious about their whereabouts, to know if they are hungry or thirsty, so I have come here. My son, you can help me find my children. Then I can go back home."

Lieutenant Şükrü felt a stirring of emotion. This old woman, like himself, was worried if anyone else had been left outside. It was as if every member of this nation had the conscience of a military leader! He kissed her hands and tried to comfort her. "Grandma, do not worry at all! No one is left outside. Go home with an easy heart!"

"Muhtar promised me, didn't he? Now I am to be left out of the good deeds? What happens when my Lord asks me on the Day of Judgment, "What did you do that night?"

Lieutenant Şükrü wanted to make the grandmother happy. He found several soldiers who had not yet gone to bed at headquarters. He sent them with the old woman. With joy, as if she had found a treasure, the grandmother led them to her house. Like a bird, she flew home. The lieutenant stared after her for a long time.

"In this land," he murmured, "as long as these mothers and their prayers continue, the enemy can never defeat us."

Feeble Mehmet

It was a mild July night. There was movement in the bushes. Turkish forces were gathering at Domuzdere, planning to make a quick sortie with bayonets against the enemy, on the outskirts of the village Kitre. The trenches of the enemy were 300 meters away.

The skirmishes continued for days. As the trenches came closer to each other, there was no possibility of progressing even a step. The soldiers of the third regiment came from behind and flowed into the trenches. In a narrow region, more than 10,000 soldiers took their places in the bushes. The enemy noticed nothing, since talking and smoking were banned. They stepped soundlessly, taking care not to disturb the dry bushes or make any noise. The soldiers proceeded like a lifeless shadow, using the darkness as a curtain. In the darkness of night, only the noises of insects were heard. The cicadas sang with a vigorous zeal, as if they wanted to support the Turkish soldiers.

After taking their places, bayonets came out of their shields silently. Still, there was no movement on the enemy's side. Noiselessly, bayonets were fastened to the ends of the rifles. The men communicated with signs. Finally, the whole regiment was prepared, ready to attack.

They were waiting for the order to attack. There was a mood of overwhelming excitement. In a short while, Domuzdere would be like Doomsday. As the moments passed, the feeling in the soldiers' chests was turning into flames of fire. The fervor of Feeble Mehmet was more than the others.

His friends called him *çelimsiz* (feeble) because his body was frail. What his friends meant was that he was no good for anything, which offended him very much. His chest was expanding and shrinking like an accordion. His giant heart was too heavy for his weak body. Often when gazing through the spaces between sand bags at the enemy lines, he grew restless. Turning to the commander beside him, he whispered: "My commander! Permit me to take my place at the head of the left column."

His commander made a gesture that meant: "What are you going to do?"

"I cannot tell you that now," he murmured. "Just give me permission."

The commander felt decisiveness in the voice of Feeble Mehmet, and did not make him repeat himself. In a moment, thousands of men were going run forward, attacking the enemy. How could it be important for one man to be at this end or the other? It was easy for the commander to read the newfound self-confidence in Feeble Mehmet's eyes.

So he nodded: "Okay, go ahead."

Mehmet moved to take his new place. It was still half-way dark. On every tongue, there was silent movement. Five minutes before the attack, the level of excitement reached its climax. Five minutes to the attack also meant five minutes to martyrdom. Every heart was beating like a machine gun.

The time was 3:45, attack time. All of a sudden, waves of Turkish soldiers, platoon after platoon, jumped from their trenches. As the first platoons plunged into the enemy line, an uproar began. On the hill enemy soldiers must have been ready at the machine gun, because in moments it started to rain death all around.

The Turkish soldiers threw themselves into the pits, underneath bushes. It was like Doomsday. Some skirmished in the trenches, others ran forward under the fire of the machine guns, and still others were tasting the syrup of martyrdom.

The machine gun had to be silenced. Otherwise, many patriotic youth would die without any military gain. From where he lay, Feeble Mehmet focused his eyes on the hill, waiting for it to stop even for a moment, in order to stand up. The machine gun was hidden in a trench unaffected by the Turkish soldiers' fire. Suddenly, he shouted to his commander: "My commander! Cover my rear!"

Feeble Mehmet, taking no notice of the machine gun, slithered quietly to the hill. Although his friends had started firing in that direction of the beast, it never fell silent. The battlefield was slipping out of its dark garment. Feeble Mehmet had forgotten death. The commander understood him now.

His jeering comrades were now spectators full of admiration and envy as he crawled with no fear for his life. As he slithered underneath the machine gun, he shook the bipod. The gun jolted and lost its target. Its barrel fired toward the sky. At that moment, shouting "Allah, Allah!" his friends jumped from their trenches and launched an attack. The gun's silence and the soldiers' shout spurred other squads to do the same. That moment changed the destiny of the battle.

QUESTIONS

1) "The Companions' success lies in a universal language which they spoke. This language was the _____." Which best fills in the blank?

    A) language of conduct and good manners

    B) sign language

    C) body language

    D) local language

2) How many verses did Mus'ab ibn Umayr know when he went to Medina?

    A) 10   C) 12

    B) 11   D) 13

3) After staying in Medina for one year, how many people did Mus'ab ibn Umayr bring to Aqaba to pledge allegiance?

    A) 65   C) 73

    B) 72   D) 82

4) Which country is the subject of the article, "How Does a White Man Serve an African?"

    A) Kenya   C) Nigeria

    B) Madagascar   D) South Africa

5) In the article "As Long as Such Mothers Are Alive," what is the name of the settlement where the 33rd Regiment camped?

    A) Edremit   C) Ezine

    B) Conk Bayırı   D) Havran

6) In the article, "Feeble Mehmet," where did the great heroism take place?

    A) Bedre   C) Kitre

    B) Sav   D) Eskişehir

7) In the article "As Long as Such Mothers Are Alive," why did the old woman met wander in the pitch dark on the streets, and say to the commander, "Now I am to be left out of the good deeds?"

A) not being able to participate in the war

B) not being able to host soldiers in her home at night

C) not being able to carry provisions to the front

D) not being able to provide additional ammunition to the front

8) Where did Mus'ab ibn Umayr pay allegiance to our noble Prophet with the Medinese that he had persuaded?

A) Mecca   C) Uhud

B) Taif   D) Aqaba

9) "Starting in _____ 1999 with a Turkish channel, various cassette recordings were broadcast, one after another. The conversations, which contained no criminal elements, were spliced together to provoke a wave of indignation and outrage among the public." Which best fills in the blank?

A) June   C) August

B) July   D) September

CHAPTER 8

OUR NOBLE PROPHET

Why Are We Supposed to Love Our Noble Prophet More than All Other Creatures?

Prophet Muhammad, peace and blessings be upon him, is a blessed guide for human beings to come to enlightenment, from *kufr* (disbelief) into *iman* (faith, belief), because he is the most beautiful example, the excellent model of conduct for the believers. What is more natural than for believers to love the one who did them so much good?

The All-Compassionate asked the believers to love His beloved, Muhammad, peace and blessings be upon him: "*Say: If your fathers and your sons, your brothers and your spouses and your clans. Together with the wealth you acquired and a commerce you fear will find no market, and homes you find pleasing—if all these are dearer to you than God, his Messenger and the struggle in his cause, then wait until God fulfills his decree. God guides not the dissolute*" (at-Tawbah 9:24). Anas may Allah be pleased with him, narrated: "The Messenger of Allah said: 'None of you will have faith till he loves me more than his father, his children and all mankind.'" (*Sahih al-Bukhari*, Book 2, Hadith 8).

The sincere, heartfelt love of the believers for the noble Prophet also allows them to taste the spiritual pleasure of loving. When this love is absent, they would be deprived of the pleasure of submission and faith, and they would be in the situation of the one who eats without the sense of taste. In the next life, believers want to meet Muhammad Mustafa, peace and blessings be upon him, the Pride of Humankind.

The Compass of Believers

All the religious practices we are required to perform include the Sunnah, the practice of the Prophet. The beautiful practice of the Prophet is based upon his words, actions, and approvals, and it represents his moral values and lifestyle. He says, "Whoever tries to resemble me, he belongs to my tradition." In this respect, the Sunnah of the Prophet is the compass of believers, which always points to the truth. His behavior and attitude is chosen by God as the Prophet states, "My Lord has taught and educated me, and how well He has taught and educated me!" It is difficult to find one's way if one does not follow this compass.

The following are some examples of the Sunnah of the Prophet, who said, "Whoever follows my Sunnah when my Community is corrupted, there is for him (or her) the reward of a hundred martyrs."

- He recited "Bismillah" (In the Name of God, the All-Merciful, the All-Compassionate) before doing anything.
- He entered and left home by greeting.
- He knocked the door of a house three times at most.
- He perfumed himself with beautiful scents.
- He used a brush-like tool called "siwak" to clean his teeth.
- He did not let anyone down when they asked something from him.
- He visited his friends and relatives.
- He hosted his guests with clean clothes and served them whatever he had on hand.

- He accepted when he was invited by someone.
- He offered his condolences to people who lost their friends or families.
- He participated in Funeral Prayers.
- He visited the sick.
- He offered his Daily Prayers in congregation.
- He played and joked with children.
- He always advised the right.
- He washed his hands before and after meals.
- He recited *Bismillah* before he began eating and ended with grace.
- He accepted gifts and reciprocated those gifts with equal or superior gifts.
- He remembered the deceased in good terms.
- He helped those who prepared to get married.
- He held good assumptions about people unless otherwise proven.
- He supported those who were seeking knowledge and receiving education.
- He congratulated newly married couples.
- He covered his mouth with his hand when he sneezed.
- He brought his palms together, recited specific verses from the Qur'an (al-Ikhlas, al-Falaq, an-Nas) before he went to bed and wiped his palms to his body.
- He lied on the right hand side when he went to sleep, pulled his legs closer to his body, he put his right hand's palm onto his right cheek and contemplated the day.
- He did not sleep in a facedown position.

- He recited *Bismillah* before he drank water and finished drinking in three steps. He also said *Alhamdulillah* (All praise be to Allah) after he drank.
- He drank Zamzam water (a famous well very near the Ka'ba in Mecca) standing up and facing the Ka'ba.
- He tinged his eyes with kohl three times every night.
- If something grieved him, he would offer Prayers.
- He took ablution before each and every Prayer.
- He visited graves.
- He made peace between people.
- He prayed very often and always repented.
- He endured with patience during times of disaster.
- He put his clothes on from the right side and took them off from the left side.

What Kind of Humor Did Our Noble Prophet Have?

Our dear Prophet treated people sincerely, from his heart. From time to time, he made some jokes. In his presence was a comfortable atmosphere. If it was otherwise, people would not have felt close to him, they could not have asked him questions.

One cannot solely talk about heavy and serious matters. Sometimes the atmosphere must be softened so people feel relaxed. Our noble Prophet made jokes, but he never lied. If it is jokingly a lie, it is still a lie. The Messenger of Allah never made fun of people, did not belittle or denigrate. He never embarrassed people or put them on the spot. He did not approve of practical jokes or pulling someone's legs.

Here is an example. Anas, may Allah be pleased with him, narrated: "A man coming to the Messenger of Allah said: 'O Messenger of Allah! Mount me on a camel.' He said: 'I will mount you on the baby of a camel.' The man said: 'O Messenger of Allah! What will I do with the baby of a camel?' The Prophet replied: "Was a camel born out of another creature? Isn't every camel the baby of another camel?'"

With this joke, our noble Prophet also taught a lesson: One should never hurry to reject something at once, without thinking deeply and comprehending its content in full.

In these two incidences, we see examples of jokes he made with children. Our noble Prophet used to visit Anas and his family from time to time. Anas's brother, Umayr, had a bird named al-Nughayr. On one of these visits, the Prophet said, "O Abu Umayr, what happened to al-Nughayr?" By referring to the boy as "father," he made a jest, and yet also showed interest in his concerns. He also joked with Anas by calling him "the one with two ears!" His humor was always aimed at guidance, the establishment of close ties or love, or erasing sadness and grief.

One day, when an old lady asked him for a prayer to enter Paradise, our beloved Prophet gravely replied, "Old ladies cannot enter Paradise." The lady became very downcast at this answer, and he smiled and said: "Didn't you know that all will be young when they enter Paradise?" His was a subtle humor that also counseled and comforted.

UMRAH

Qur'anic Verses

Behold, the first House (of Prayer) established for humankind is the one at Bakkah (Mecca), a blessed place and a (center or focus of) guidance for all peoples. In it there are clear signs (demonstrating that it is a blessed sanctuary, chosen by God as the center of guidance), and the Station of Abraham. Whoever enters it is in security (against attack and fear). Pilgrimage to the House is a duty owed to God by all who can afford a way to it. And whoever refuses (the obligation of the Pilgrimage) or is ungrateful to God (by not fulfilling this command), God is absolutely independent of all creatures. (Al Imran 3:96-97).

(The hills of) as-Safa and Marwa are among the emblems God has appointed (to represent Islam and the Muslim community). Hence whoever does the Hajj (the Major Pilgrimage) to the House (of God, the Ka'ba) or the *Umrah* (the Minor Pilgrimage), there is no blame on him to run between them (and let them run after they go round the Ka'ba as an obligatory rite). And whoever does a good work voluntarily (such as additional going-round the Ka'ba and running between as-Safa and Marwa, and other kinds of good works) surely God is All-Responsive to thankfulness, All-Knowing. (Al-Baqarah 2:158).

Invitation from the Sultan of the Hearts

The noble Prophet said: "If you visit the Ka'ba and perform jihad (striving in God's cause and for humanity's good), you will become the envoy of God. Because God invited you to do those things and you obeyed His desire. God will certainly give what you want from Him."

Circumambulation of the Ka'ba

The Messenger of Allah said: "Circumambulation of the Ka'ba is an important worship like the Daily Prayers. While doing it, talk right things."

The Most Beneficial Water

The last Prophet said: "The most beneficial water is *Zamzam*. It is a relieving cure for patients. For whatever reason it is drunk, it gives a cure for it."

The Most Important Worship of Women

One day our dear mother Aisha asked the Messenger of Allah: "O Messenger of Allah, we know that the most important worship is jihad. Do we have to perform jihad as women?"

God's Messenger replied: "For women the most important worship is Hajj (pilgrimage to Mecca)."

Drinking Zamzam

I was sitting with Ibn Abbas when another man came. Ibn Abbas asked him where he was coming from.

The man said: "I came from the Zamzam source."

Ibn Abbas asked: "Have you drunk it as it was required?"

The man asked: "How could I do this?"

Ibn Abbas explained: "While drinking Zamzam, turn to the *qiblah* (the direction of Mecca) and say *Bismillah* (In the Name of Allah). After you drink it, thank God. Because the Messenger said

that the difference between Muslims and unbelievers is that
unbelievers do not drink Zamzam with desire."

My Brother

Umar missed the Ka'ba very much and a great desire arose in him
to visit Mecca and the Ka'ba. He demanded permission from the
Messenger of Allah. He allowed and said: "My brother, pray for
me, too."

Umar was profoundly affected by his words. Umar loved the
noble Messenger so much. When this wonderful memory fell into
his mind, so did the tears on Umar's face.

THE LIVES OF COMPANIONS

The Man at the Summit in Loving Our Noble Prophet: Mus'ab

The people of Medina asked the Messenger of Allah to send them a teacher of religion. He sent Mus'ab, a handsome, gentle man. When Mus'ab went to Medina to prepare the city for his Prophet, he was 25 years old.

For a year, Mus'ab explained Islam to the Medinese. From time to time, he would be rebuked, and sometimes people would try to hit him. The young teacher always responded with mildness. He smiled at those who showed anger, and looked with love at those who looked with hatred. To those who turned their faces away, he extended his hands in compassion.

During the entire year, Mus'ab poured his compassion, love, mercy and patience into Medina. At the end of a year, he set out with the people of Medina to visit his Prophet.

The young Mus'ab who departed Mecca with 12 individuals, returned with 72 hearts full of faith. A year later, the Prophet came to Medina. Everything happened very fast. After a short time, the Battle of Badr took place. Despite his young age, Mus'ab was the first flag bearer at Badr.

A year later came the Battle of Uhud. Mus'ab again bore the flag. With a sword in his hand, he fought until the evening. He fought in such a way that even the angels looked at him with admiration. For a moment, from a wound he received from swords, he fell facedown on the ground. Immediately, an angel started fighting in the disguise of his body.

In the evening, the Messenger of Allah shouted, "Mus'ab!" and the angel answered, "I am not Mus'ab, O Messenger of Allah!" And all was clear. Mus'ab had been martyred hours before. After a short search, the Messenger of Allah and some Companions found the dead body of Mus'ab. Both arms were torn from the shoulders.

The All-Omnipotent had protected his religion and maintained it. This protection continued until a certain time. Afterwards, sporadically, there were tremors. During these shakings, when the religion was not lived as it ought to be, the All-Compassionate cut His blessings. This religion is what we internalize. If we do not live it, He will deprive us of it.

QUESTIONS

1) *"Say: If your fathers and your sons, your brothers and your spouses and your clans. Together with the wealth you acquired and a commerce you fear will find no market, and homes you find pleasing—if all these are dearer to you than God, his Messenger and the struggle in his cause, then wait until God fulfills his decree. God guides not the dissolute."* This verse is taken from which chapter of the Qur'an?

    A) al-Baqarah   C) Ya-Sin

    B) at-Tawbah   D) al-Furqan

2) What is "the compass of believers"?

    A) the Sunnah   C) natural sciences

    B) *Fiqh*   D) theology

3) Which of the following is not one of the Sunnah of the Prophet?

    A) starting everything with *Bismillah*

    B) making peace between people

C) eating a lot

D) visiting relatives and friends

4) "Whoever follows my Sunnah when my Community is corrupted, there is for him (or her) the reward of a _____ martyrs." Which number best fills in the blank?

A) 100   C) 300

B) 200   D) 500

5) "A man coming to the Messenger of Allah said: 'O Messenger of Allah! Mount me on a camel.' He said: 'I will mount you on the baby of a camel.' The man said: 'O Messenger of Allah! What will I do with the baby of a camel?' The Prophet replied: "Was a camel born out of another creature? Isn't every camel the baby of another camel?"'" Which Companion narrated this *hadith*?

A) Abu Hurayra   C) Anas

B) Bilal   D) Uthman

6) Which of the following is the first building constructed for worship?

A) the Quba Masjid   C) Al-Masjid al-Aqsa

B) the Ka'ba   D) the Prophet's Mosque

7) "_____ and _____ *are among the emblems God has appointed (to represent Islam and the Muslim community). Hence whoever does the Hajj (the Major Pilgrimage) to the House (of God, the Ka'ba) or the Umrah (the Minor Pilgrimage), there is no blame on him to run between them (and let them run after they go round the Ka'ba as an obligatory rite)."* Which words best fill in the blanks?

A) Badr, Uhud   C) Mecca, Medina

B) as-Safa, Marwa   D) the Ka'ba, Quba

8) Which of the following did our noble Prophet declare as the greatest jihad for women?

A) fighting in the front
C) Hajj
B) raising children
D) Tahajjud

9) The Medinese requested our beloved Prophet send someone to teach them their religion. Which young, soft-spoken, and handsome Companion did he send?

A) Muawiyah
C) Zayd
B) Bilal
D) Mus'ab

10) Which Companion was the first flag-bearer of Islam at the Battle of Badr?

A) Ali
C) Mus'ab
B) Hamza
D) Umar

CHAPTER 9

SATANIC INTRIGUES

What are the Six Human and Satanic Intrigues?

The human being has been sent to the world for examination. Life continues from beginning to end as a series of trials of differing dimensions and depths. The human being is confronted with these trials starting from their childhood, and lasting until the moment when their soul is resigned to its Lord. In the Sixth Section of "The Twenty-Ninth Letter" in *The Letters*, named "The Six Attacks", Said Nursi states, "God willing, this Sixth Section will confound six stratagems of satans among jinn and men, and block up six of their ways of attack," and as such identifies the most dangerous of these trials as the desire for rank and position, the sense of fear, greed, racialism, egotism, and love of comfort.

Now, let us try to briefly elucidate these diseases that Said Nursi has identified, again from his perspective. The desire for rank and position denotes the desire to hold a particular post or position and to be famed among the people. He summarizes this feeling within the human being as follows: "Present in most people is a hypocritical desire to be seen by people and hold a position in the public view, which is ambition for fame and acclaim, and self-advertisement; it is present to a lesser or greater extent in all those who seek this world. The desire to accomplish this ambition will drive a person to sacrifice his life even."

The desire for rank and position is an evil trait that darkens the heart and paralyzes the spirit. It is always within the realm of possibility for those unfortunate souls who have yielded their hearts to such a sickness, to have their vision blurred and deviate to dead ends. In fact, the desire for rank and position may be found more or less in every individual. It is for this reason that if the endeavor is not made to satisfy this emotion within a legitimate sphere, it is inevitable that those unable to free themselves from the clutches of such an attitude will inflict harm on both themselves and the society in which they live. Such damage is virtually irreparable.

The second is the sense of fear. A person can bridle their will-power with the bridle of fear. Especially in our day, the people of heedlessness attempt to suppress human beings with the sense of fear. Said Nursi states: "One of the strongest and most basic emotions in man is the sense of fear. Scheming oppressors profit greatly from the emotion of fear. They restrain the pusillanimous with it. The agents of the worldly and propagandists of the people of misguidance take advantage of this weak point of the common people and of the religious scholars in particular. They frighten them and excite their groundless fears." In so doing, he presents the matter with consideration of its modern elements. A heart that has believed in the truth can only be freed of this sickness by means of a spiritual attentiveness and through the conviction, "May my honor, integrity, and pride be sacrificed in this cause! Death is only in the hands of God." The sole remedy for not feeling fear of anyone is to fear the One who really deserves to be feared.

The third intrigue is greed. Greed is the excessive desire to acquire or possess something, avarice, and insatiability. With the words, "If the children of Adam possessed two valleys of gold, they would surely desire a third (valley of gold); only the soil (of the grave) can satisfy their avarice. God forgives those who turn to Him in repentance," God's Messenger depicts the psychological state of those people who are enslaved to greed. The human being can only escape the clutches of greed through taking the verse, *"Eat and drink, but do not be wasteful,"* (al-A'raf 7:31) as a standard for themselves and conducting their expenditure without tending to waste. Moreover, some evil spirits can enter through the vein of avarice and make believers instruments for their own loathsome ends. Nursi states: "Yes, 'the worldly' and especially the people of misguidance do not give away their money cheaply; they sell it at a high price. Sometimes something which may help a little towards a year of worldly life is the means of destroying infinite eternal life. And with that vile greed, the person draws Divine wrath on himself and tries to attract the pleasure of the people of misguidance." In so doing, he draws attention to such a danger.

The fourth matter is racialism. The notion of racialism first started in Europe and later became one of the agents paving the way for the end of the Ottoman State. They set the people of this nation, favored with the manifestation of "Divine coloring," against one another with the idea of racialism, Turks against Kurds, Kurds against Bosnians, Bosnians against Albanians. Islam opposes such an understanding of nationalism, which places racialism before religion.

Indeed, tribalism and racialism was completely abolished by virtue of the bond of belief in Islam. When the Companions of the Prophet are considered, it immediately becomes evident that the majority of them were from different races. For instance, Abu Bakr was an Arab, Bilal Ethiopian, Suhayb Byzantine, and Salman Persian. Despite all of them being people of differing climates and nations, they united in the melting pot of Islam and became brothers. The verse, *"Surely the noblest, most honorable of you in God's sight is the one best in piety, righteousness, and reverence for God,"* (al-Hujurat 49:13) documents this truth. As mentioned above, while Islam rejects a negative nationalism, which holds race above religion on the one hand, it on the other hand has established a positive nationalism, based on the fact family and lineage, nationhood, and people are also a reality.

This is, moreover, a social fact which is indicated in the verse, *"O humankind! Surely We have created you from a single (pair of) male and female, and made you into tribes and families so that you may know one another"* (al-Hujurat 49:13). Bediüzzaman Said Nursi has diagnosed this reality in a striking manner and has articulated it thus: "The idea of positive nationalism should serve Islam and be its citadel and armor; it should not take its place. For within the brotherhood of Islam is a hundredfold brotherhood that persists in the Intermediate Realm and World of Eternity. So whatever its extent, national brotherhood may be an element of it. But to plant it in place of Islamic brotherhood is a foolish crime like replacing the treasure of diamonds within the citadel with the citadel's stones, and throwing the diamonds away."

The fifth attack is egotism, the weakest and most dangerous in the human being, and is something that needs to be cast out of a person's character once and for all. For it is very difficult for those unfortunate ones swept up in the vortex of ego to see and recognize truth and reality and, as they are blindfolded, to walk towards their aim without going astray. Again, Said Nursi affirms: "My brothers! Beware, do not let them strike you with egotism, do not let them hunt you with it! You should know that this century the people of misguidance have mounted the ego and are galloping through the valleys of misguidance. The people of truth have to give it up if they are to serve the truth. Even if a person is justified in making use of the ego, since he will resemble the others and they too will suppose he is self-seeking like them, it will be an injustice to the service of the truth. In any event, the service of the Qur'an around which we are gathered does not accept the 'I', it requires the 'we.' It says: "Don't say 'I', say 'we.'" Thus, he invites us to be on guard towards this satanic characteristic.

The sixth attack is that which encumbers as a serious sickness in a great many heroes who have devoted themselves to the truth in our day, the sickness of laziness and the desire for physical comfort. Indeed, these enlightened souls who awaken the social spirit, guide the people and elevate them to true humanity, and who are devotees of the truth, must be prepared to sacrifice everything, material or spiritual, for the sake of this ideal without ever stooping to laziness. There is a story told of legend, regarding Prophet Abraham's wealth. Whilst its authenticity may be dubious, the lesson to be taken from it is significant. Prophet Abraham owned so many sheep that had so many shepherds that he is considered to be among the wealthiest in regard to his day. Some of the angels, who could not reconcile such great wealth with the office of Prophethood—notwithstanding the particular notion that it sprang from—directed the following question: "How can all this wealth be compatible with the position of Prophethood?" God Almighty then declared: "Has this wealth entered his heart or not? Go and test him!" Upon this, the angels, under the command of the angel of Revelation Archangel Gabriel, appeared in human form and went to the presence of Prophet Abraham. Here, the angels uttered the words, "Transcendent and Holy You Are, the Lord of the angels and the Spirit," loud enough for him to hear, as an expression of their knowledge of God. These words are carefully selected, in way of exaltation and glorification of God Almighty. With a heart receptive to breezes from the Divine Realm, Prophet Abraham was immensely pleased when he heard such glorification and articulated his astonishment with the words, "For God's sake, what a beautiful thing this is! May one third of my wealth be yours, repeat your words once more!" When the angels repeated the statement, Prophet Abraham said: "Let half of it be yours!" When they repeated it a third time, however, he responded saying, "I am bound in servitude to you, along with my shepherds!" Upon this, Archangel Gabriel introduced himself and said: "I am one of God's angels. I do not need any of these; however, my Lord desired to display your faithfulness and tested you with us." The angels then left. The travelers upon the path of truth must perpetually continue along their way and be wary of being swept up in the vortex of ease and comfort, despite having the approval of God as their sole intention.

In short, gazes must constantly be directed towards God in return for His infinite mercy, without losing hope in and regard for Him for even an instant, and one must act satiated with a sense of self-control and supervision. In this way, the spirit of action will not be atrophied and, by not being swept up by the intrigues known as the "Six Attacks" and through becoming freed of the shame of sins and drinking to repletion the celestial waters of forgiveness, it will be possible to reach the infinite mercy which gives relief to spirits.

COMPASSIONATE PUNISHMENT

What Does the Term "Blows Dealt by Divine Compassion" Tell Us?

Compassionate punishment is a sweet warning for the beloved to bring him back to the right path, akin to a gentle tug on a child's ear to rebuke him. Bediüzzaman places significance on compassionate punishment and on "The Tenth Gleam" under the light of the following verse: "*On that day humans will face everything they did, as good deeds or bad deeds, and they will wish for some distance between themselves and their bad deeds. Allah the Almighty is warning those who revolt against Him. He is compassionate towards His servants*" (Al Imran 3:30), he explains this matter with the then available examples.

Blows dealt by Divine Compassion take place according to the place one has in the eyes of the One Who slaps, and takes shape accordingly. Take for instance the person who believes but does not have a serious personal relationship with Allah the Almighty. When he has a fault in his obligatory Prayers or a contrary belief, may experience a compassionate slap in the form of a loss in family or wealth. Such a slap could be a vehicle for him to learn a lesson or step back onto the right path. When looked at from this perspective, there is no doubt that it is a blessing and a gift.

Consider a person who wakes up in the darkest hour of the night to put his forehead on the Prayer rug, and who sheds many tears for the Hereafter. If he neglects a night, the next morning he will feel black clouds roaming inside his mind until evening. For a person at this level, the clouds are blows dealt by Divine Compassion. Because the All-Merciful has elevated him and, so to speak, brought him to the deck of the ship. For one who has been in charge of the deck of the ship, saying, "I will feed the coal" or "I will be fold the sailing cloth" will be a degradation. Allah does not approve such a fall; because of His mercy, He gives a compassionate slap so that he will come back to himself.

We witness blows dealt by Divine Compassion during the time of the Companions. The Messenger of Allah put forward the suggestion of staying in Medina to consult before the Battle of Uhud. But the young Companions, who made up the majority, wanted to make an offensive war. They were very sincere in this opinion, with no intention apart from showing the enemy his place.

This sincere intention was the cause of the revelation of this verse: "*Among the believers are men (of highest valor) who have been true to their covenant with God: among them are those who have fulfilled their vow (by remaining steadfast until death), and those who are awaiting (its fulfillment). They have never altered in any way*" (al-Ahzab 33:23). However, the passion and zeal of the Companions prevented them from understanding the finesse and subtlety of obedience to the order.

In addition, archers who had been charged with guarding the rear flank had left their places. Despite a direct order from the Prophet: "Protect our rear and do not, under any circumstances, leave your places. Even if you see us sharing the booty, do not leave. Again, even if eagles come and pick at our torsos, remain in your places!" Still, they left their places.

In partial defeat, and for tactical reasons, the Muslim army was to retreat. This, too, was a compassionate slap. The Companions who understood the warning immediately gathered around the noble Prophet and, following the enemy, they transformed their sin into a good deed and their defeat into a victory.

For the modern travelers of truth who give their hearts to the cause of the blessed Prophet, blows dealt by Divine Compassion will abound, for this is the most honorable path. Remembering the straight path is the most important thing.

If there were something more important, the All-Merciful would have charged His Prophet with that duty. What makes Gabriel so exalted, extending his head to the highest heavens, is being charged with this duty. So, even if it is small, any behavior which would harm a person could cause this, according to his status, and his consciousness of his responsibility.

No one has the right to sacrifice even a tiny portion of this sublime ideal. The Messenger of Allah fulfilled everything he was charged with. A verse commands: "O Messenger (you who convey and embody the Message in the best way)! Convey and make known in the clearest way all that has been sent down to you from your Lord. For, if you do not, you have not conveyed His Message and fulfilled the task of His Messengership. And God will certainly protect you from the people" (al-Maedah 5:67). And so he carried out this requirement to the fullest extent.

Afterwards, prominent figures such as Umar ibn Abdulaziz, al-Ghazali, al-Jilani, Imam Sirhindi, Mawlana Khalid al-Bahghdadi, and Bediüzzaman took this duty upon themselves. In their respective periods, they explained the blows dealt by Divine Compassion in the best possible manner.

In our times, those who seek this sublime ideal and preoccupation should not give any place in their service to the laziness and negligence of their people. Otherwise, the compassionate slap is inevitable. Recognizing the value of a blessing is a vehicle for new blessings. This is possible only through thanksgiving for every blessing and searching for ways to increase these blessings.

TRUST AND RELIANCE
ON ALLAH

Resigning Oneself to Allah the Almighty

Thousands of experiences prove that no matter how many efforts are made toward a goal, it is possible for it all to go up in smoke. What is up to us is to work tooth and nail; but afterward, we must resign the outcome to Allah the Almighty (Fethullah Gülen).

What is *Tawakkul?*

Tawakkul means leaving an outcome up to Allah with complete confidence and faith, after having made every effort and taken every precaution. *Tawakkul* in any matter, worldly or otherworldly, means doing the work toward a goal, but leaving the consequence to Allah.

The verse, *"When two parties of you were about to lose heart, although God was their helper and protector and in God, let the believers put all their trust"* (Al Imran 3:122) denotes this concept. Our noble Prophet advises the believers to have *tawakkul*: "If you all depend on Allah with due reliance, He would certainly give you provision as He gives it to the birds that go forth hungry in the morning and return with full bellies at dusk."

Since *tawakkul* is a state related to the heart, working manually and earning a livelihood is not against *tawakkul* or a barrier to it. This is simply performing the physical duties of servanthood, an opportunity to be grateful for one's basic needs being met.

Trust in Allah means finding Him sufficient at all times—in the blessings and disasters, in the comfort and troubles that He has chosen for one. The rightness of something, in terms of its consequences, is often concealed from human beings. But we know the thing Allah chooses for a human being is better than what he chooses for himself. *Tawakkul* is complete confidence in and submission to His preference. Its sign is being patient and even thankful in the face of calamities and disasters.

Some Remarks on *Tawakkul*

Imam Fakhruddin ar-Razi says: "*Tawakkul* does not mean, as some uneducated people think, that people neglect themselves. If it was so, the command to consult with each other would've been an obstacle for *tawakkul*. *Tawakkul* means complying with the external appearances of cause and effect, but not attaching your heart to them and instead taking refuge in the Almighty God."

* * *

After having constructed the best ship and having sailed through the ocean and reached the shore, we must know this as God's gift and praise and thank Him because a ship's perfection and a captain's expertise cannot stand against those mountain-like waves and probable storms.

Making the ship perfect is an example of placing effort into causality. After having completed this commitment, *tawakkul* is leaving the outcome after having left the shore to God's grace.

* * *

A parable is usually explained: Prophet Sulayman, peace be upon him, inquires as to how much an ant eats in the course of a year. "A grain of wheat," they replied. To test this, he put an ant in a box and threw in a grain of wheat.

A year later he opens the box and sees that the ant has eaten only half of the wheat. He asks the ant: "Don't you eat a whole grain of wheat a year?" The ant responds: "O Sulayman! That was when my sustenance was provided by the All-Providing, the All-Munificent. But when you began to provide for my sustenance, I did not know what you would do in the future. What if you forgot me? However, my Lord never forgets any being among His creation. That's why I acted with caution," the ant said.

SENSITIVITY REGARDING THE PROHIBITED AND THE LAWFUL

Numan ibn Bashir narrates: "I heard the Messenger of Allah say, 'What is lawful is clear and what is unlawful is (also) clear. But between the two are doubtful matters of which many people do not know. He who protects himself from doubtful matters clears himself in regard to his faith and honor. But he who falls into doubtful matters is like a shepherd who grazes (his sheep) around a sanctuary, and (liable) to graze therein. Surely, every king has a sanctuary. Surely, the sanctuary of God is His prohibitions. Surely, in the body is a piece of flesh, and if it is sound, the whole body is sound; and if it is damaged, the body is diseased. Surely, it is the heart.'" (*Sahih al-Bukhari*, Iman, 39)

What Do Lawful and Prohibited (*Halal* and *Haram*) Mean?

Halal defines that which is not prohibited in the Islamic faith, whereas *haram* defines that which is not lawful.

That which has not been defined as prohibited is permissible. God revealed: "*It is He Who created all that is in the world for you*" (al-Baqarah 2:29) "*Do you not see that God has made all that is in the heavens and all that is on the earth of service to you*" (Luqman 31:20). These verses of the Qur'an state that God created many blessings for mankind. That which was not prohibited to eat, drink or use in the Qur'an and Traditions of the noble Prophet are permissible, and that prohibited is unlawful.

In this chapter, we will be discussing and analyzing the prohibitions and lawful aspects of food, drink, clothing, household goods, the fields of work and income, occupation and transactions which exist in both the family and social lives, and generally aspects which mainly concern the younger members of the Islamic faith.

The Prohibited and Lawful Aspects Regarding Food and Drink

Complying with certain conditions, all foods and drinks, with the exception of those stipulated in the Qur'an, are stated as being permissible, in addition, it also states that nobody has the right to render what God has deemed prohibited as permissible, or what God has deemed permissible as prohibited. One of the points emphasized in the Qur'an is that sustenance should be "lawful and pure." Even if these foods are lawful, the Qur'an still forbids excessiveness and waste in terms of eating and drinking.

One of the main aims in forbidding certain foods and drinks is to maintain the physical and spiritual health of humans. The substances which are proved to be damaging to the human body both physically and spiritually are classified forbidden in the Islamic faith. Substances which have an intoxicating effect are also among the things prohibited in Islam.

QUESTIONS

1) Which of the following is not one of the six tricks of Satan?
   A) desire for public recognition and fame
   B) fear
   C) greed
   D) death

2) Desire for status and fame is expressed by which of the following?

   A) racism   C) love of status
   B) greed   D) laziness

3) Which of the following is Satan's trick for desiring something with over-ambition, greed and non-satiation?

   A) egotism   C) love of status
   B) greed   D) laziness

4) "The notion of racialism first started in _____." Which best fills in the blank?

   A) USA   C) Europe
   B) Asia   D) Middle East

5) In which battle did our noble Prophet make the following warning: "Protect our rear and do not, under any circumstances, leave your places. Even if you see us sharing the booty, do not leave. Again, even if eagles come and pick at our torsos, remain in your places!"?

   A) Uhud   C) Trench
   B) Badr   D) Hunayn

6) After making every necessary effort, and taking every precaution, what is the name of leaving a matter to Allah in complete faith?

   A) *tafakkur*   C) *tawakkul*
   B) *qadar*   D) modesty

7) Prophet Sulayman, peace be upon him, checked which animal's obedience to the principle of *tawakkul*?

A) cats

C) locusts

B) lions

D) ants

8) "_____ defines that which is not prohibited in the Islamic faith, whereas _____ defines that which is not lawful." Which set of words best fills in the blanks?

A) *Haram, halal*

C) *Jaiz, halal*

B) *Halal, haram*

D) *Haram, jaiz*

9) "I heard the Messenger of Allah say, 'What is lawful is clear and what is unlawful is (also) clear. But between the two are doubtful matters of which many people do not know. He who protects himself from doubtful matters clears himself in regard to his faith and honor. But he who falls into doubtful matters is like a shepherd who grazes (his sheep) around a sanctuary, and (liable) to graze therein. Surely, every king has a sanctuary. Surely, the sanctuary of God is His prohibitions. Surely, in the body is a piece of flesh, and if it is sound, the whole body is sound; and if it is damaged, the body is diseased. Surely, it is the heart.'" Which Companion narrated this *hadith* from the Messenger of Allah?

A) Numan ibn Bashir

C) Abu Akil

B) Zayd ibn Haritha

D) Talha ibn Ubaydullah

10) After his life, the duty of the Messenger was continued and shouldered by the Companions and the scholars of the centuries. Who among the following is not a scholar?

A) Umar ibn Abdulaziz

C) Mawlana Khalid al-Baghdadi

B) Imam Sirhindi

D) Yunus Emre

CHAPTER 10

ALTRUISM

Our History Is Ample with Such Fidelity and Altruism

J ust like in the Age of Happiness, the lives of our glorious forefathers who had taken the Companions as an example to themselves have also produced many pictures of fidelity and altruism.

National Resistance is the name of a struggle of fight to death. During this fight to death, the people of Anatolia had written a legendary story of revival as they defended this beautiful land which has been kneaded for centuries with the sound of *adhan*, from the enemy boots that tried to march on it.

In this battle to protect the rosy color of our flag from fading, we see many Mehmetçiks, Ayşeciks and Fatmacıks whose natural disposition have been molded with gallantry. Most of them are the unknown heroes of this people.

It was during those days that the earth squirted martyrs and many suns had set for the sake of a crescent. It was a period in which we observe the boiling of Anatolia and a feverish action taking place all over the land. Everyone is at the front lines, from a grey-bearded old man to a young man whose facial hair has not grown yet. Indeed, anyone who is able to hold a gun was there. There was only one objective: To prevent this land from an invasion. However, this mission was difficult as it needed blood, sweat and tears.

In this Anatolia of scarcity where everyone had taken on a duty depending on their ability, one of our mothers, whose name is memorized by the inhabitants of the heavens, was running from one front to the other as she carried ammunitions to our soldiers. She would not even stop to think about her feeble and weak body as she moved continuously.

It was on one freezing morning in Kastamonu where the soldiers at the military barracks woke up to an astonishing scene. This saintly woman was standing outside with her hands raised in a position as if she was praying. She was not moving. It was a surprising picture; what was she doing outside in freezing conditions of the morning? As few soldiers walked towards the old woman to invite her inside so that she could warm herself, they came face to face with an incredible reality. This saintly woman, whose eyes pierced through your soul, had used the only blanket she had, to cover the ammunition thus she had frozen to death with her arms raised like a statue.

Later, they asked who she was but no one knew her identity. The only information they could get their hands on was that she was a woman from the village of Şeydiler. Like many other noble but unknown heroes, they entrusted her body to the bosom of this sanctified land.

The common name of these unsung heroes was Mehmetçik hence many noble women like her had rushed to the frontlines and struggled with blood and tears to serve their nation. Then without being rewarded for their services, they dispersed the seeds of spring and went away as unknown Fatmacıks and Ayşeciks.

Let us provide another example: It was a rainy autumn night in 1915. The Gallipoli Campaign had been won but the war with seven different nations who had their eyes on the sacred values of this nation continued. The city of Bilecik, the emergence point of the great Ottoman State which was once dubbed as "The Eternal State" was hosting a different kind of activity. A group of young men whose facial hair had not even grown yet were boarding a train with an intention to fight the foreigners who had come to invade their land.

The whistle signifying that the train was about to move had blown and the station became extremely active. The lighting that kept on striking was brightening the silhouette of an old Turkish mother. This woman who stood in the rain and cold with determination was noticed by the military commander Abdülkadir Bey who felt a sense of respect and admiration for her. Quickly he ran towards her and asked if she needed anything. The old woman straightened up like a soldier and explained that she was the mother of Hüseyin the son of Mehmet from the village of Akgünlü and added that she had come to see her lion off the battle.

The commander wished to get the prayer of this sanctified woman whose face had collected centuries of burdens. Quickly he summoned for Hüseyin. The young man came running and grabbed the blessed hands of his mother.

The despaired mother embraced her son for one last time with great passion and compassion and then made the following historical statement: "Hüseyin, my brave son; your uncle was martyred at Şıpka, your father at Dömeke and just eight months ago, your brothers were martyred at Çanakkale. You are my last fragment! However, I will not bless the milk I had given to you if the sound of *adhan* ceases from the minarets and if the lamps of the mosques go out. Give your life and do not return! If you pass from Şıpka, do not forget to recite al-Fatiha to your uncle. May God help you on your journey!"

This is an advice given by a mother to her only living son. The commander was frozen like a statue upon hearing these words from this blessed mother. He asked "Was all your family members martyred?"

The reply given by this mother who should be a crown on our heads had sent shivers down the spine of the commander: "Not just my family... for the past fifty years; our village cemetery had not witnessed the burial of a man. So what if we all die, let our nation survive!" She was an Anatolian mother.

Let us give an example of another unnamed mother who lived in the same era: It was a period in which our blessed nation was facing one calamity after another. There was smell of blood and gun powder all around land. From young men to girls who prepared for their weddings and from old men to grandmothers, everyone had sworn an oath to fight for their nation until the days promised by God would come.

It was in one of these days we hear the squeaking sound of an ox-cart. It is as if the wheels were screaming out the words, "Do not let dirty hands touch my sacred land!" It was the region of İnebolu and a mother walking bare feet was carrying her child in a blanket as she pulled on her ox-cart which was loaded with ammunition. Her feet which were covered in corns were making historical marks on this blessed land.

This was a unique picture no artist could ever depict. Suddenly, the drops of mercy began to turn into heavy rain as if it was giving the news of a joyous spring. What followed had made the picture even more remarkable. The mother removed the blanket from the tiny body of her baby and covered the ammunition so that it did not get wet. O Lord, what kind of a faith is this!

I do know if angels gathered to protect the baby from the heavy rain but a few hours later, they reached a public house in Ilgaz. It was the middle of the night.

A weak hand knocked on the huge doors and shouted: "Open the doors!"

A few minutes later the owner of the hotel replied: "There is no room!"

The woman shouted again and uttered something that would be written in the books of history with golden letters: "I can sleep outside with my baby but you must take the ammunition in and keep it in a safe place!"

These were the mothers who gave birth to the legendry Mehmetçiks who defended out nation.

It was during those days that the door of Cemal Bey, who was the governor of one of our border cities, was being knocked by the gendarme in the late hours of the night. As he opened the door a soldier informed him that a woman from a village which was divided between Russia and Turkey was requesting to be accepted as a refugee. She was refusing to go back no matter how much they had insisted.

They brought the poor woman into the governor's office and as soon as she saw Cemal Bey, she fell onto her knees and began to beg. She was weeping as she explained her story. Upon hearing the things she was explaining, Cemal Bey's admiration and respect for this woman began to increase by the minute.

This mother, who has been molded with the mentality of her people and religion, was pregnant. She had concealed her pregnancy for seven months, hiding in the mountains and eating leaves and grass. A few days before her due date for birth, she crossed the border into Turkish territory.

Her only wish was to give birth to her child in her mother land and then leave her baby to the authorities and go back. If she stayed in the Russian territory, her baby would be taken by the Russian authorities.

A mother whose heart was burning with such a noble desire could not be turned away hence the governor did what was necessary and accepted her refugee status. The virtuous mother delivered her baby within a week and after embracing her child for a while she gave him to the authorities and returned her village.

Yes, these mothers who sent their beloved children to the frontlines in those days are again sending their sons and daughters all over the world. How fortunate are these heroes of compassion!

WAFA (LOYALTY, FIDELITY, FAITHFULNESS)

The Messenger of Allah Was
the Exemplary Model for *Wafa*

The Messenger of Allah was the perfect model of fidelity. Keeping his word, never going back on his promises, never forgetting help he or his Companions received, visiting his friends frequently to ask how they are doing, remembering his deceased relatives, and making sacrifices for his community, all demonstrate his fidelity. This virtue alone should suffice to prove his authenticity as a Prophet.

Our noble Prophet never forgot any favor done for him. By reciprocating goodness with goodness, he showed his fidelity. One time the ambassadors of Abyssinia came into his presence. Our noble Prophet, paid close attention to them and treated them well. Some of the Companions said: "O Messenger of Allah! We will serve, please take a rest!" But our noble Prophet responded to his Companions by saying: "These people gave a place to my Companions who migrated to Abyssinia. In return, I must serve them personally."

He often recalled, mentioned, and prayed for the *Ansar* (the Helpers) who opened up their homes to him. To the *Ansar* concerned after the conquest of Mecca that he would remain in Mecca, he said, "My life as well as my death will be in your place." In this he showed once more his faithfulness to the Muslims of Medina. In doing so, he erased their concerns and comforted their hearts.

QUESTIONS

1) During the War of Independence in Kastamonu, a heroic Turkish woman spread her blanket on the ammunition instead of herself so that it wouldn't be damaged during the cold night. By morning, she had become a frozen statue. In which village did this hero freeze to death?

A) Hacılar

C) Sazoluğu

B) Çapar

D) Şeydiler

2) "Hüseyin, my brave son; your uncle was martyred at Şıpka, your father at Dömeke and just eight months ago, your brothers were martyred at Çanakkale. You are my last fragment! However, I will not bless the milk I had given to you if the sound of *adhan* ceases from the minarets and if the lamps of the mosques go out. Give your life and do not return! If you pass from Şıpka, do not forget to recite al-Fatiha to your uncle. May God help you on your journey!" During the War of Independence, in which city did this lesson for us take place?

A) Sakarya

C) Bilecik

B) Kastamonu

D) Bursa

3) For whom did the Messenger of Allah say, "My life as well as my death will be in your place"?

A) the *Muhajir*

C) the *Tabiun*

B) the *Ansar*

D) Abyssinian

4) Our noble Prophet said: "These people gave a place to my Companions who migrated to _____. In return, I must serve them personally." Which of the following should be in the blank place?

A) Mecca

C) Abyssinia

B) Medina

D) Damascus

5) What does the *Ansar* mean?

A) the Helpers

C) the Meccans

B) the Migrants

D) the Workers

ADDITIONAL
TOPICS

ETIQUETTE AND
MANNERS

Qur'anic Verses

And of those whom We have created there are people who, (in due recognition of God with His Names,) guide by the truth (by God's leave) and dispense justice by it. (Al-A'raf, 7:181).

O you who believe! Be upholders and standard-bearers of right for God's sake, being witnesses for (the establishment of) absolute justice. And by no means let your detestation for a people (or their detestation for you) move you to (commit the sin of) deviating from justice. Be just: this is nearer and more suited to righteousness and piety. Seek righteousness and piety and always act in reverence for God. Surely God is fully aware of all that you do. (Al-Maedah 5:8).

Recite and convey to them what is revealed to you of the Book, and establish the Prayer in conformity with its conditions. Surely, the Prayer restrains from all that is indecent and shameful, and all that is evil. Surely God's remembrance is the greatest (of all types of worship and not restricted to the Prayer). God knows all that you do. (Al-Ankabut 29:45).

Prophetic Traditions

Islamic Morality

God's Messenger said: "Each religion has a morality and the morality of Islam is *haya* (modesty, bashfulness)."

He said: "Bad manners and rudeness make everything nasty but morals makes everything acceptable."

The Messenger of Allah said: "If a person controls his or her anger, he or she will certainly have good deeds."

The Caliph Carrying a Sack

The caliph Umar used to wander in disguise at night in the streets of Medina to see if people needed anything and to maintain the welfare of the people.

One day, as he was on his way home along with his assistant, Aslam, after a long day of work late at night, Aslam told the Caliph:

"Isn't it cold tonight?"

Umar responded:

"Yes, indeed it is."

Umar suddenly noticed a fire in the distance and asked Aslam:

"Aslam, do you see that fire over there?"

"Yes, I do," replied Aslam.

"I wonder who set that fire," said Umar.

"I have no idea," responded Aslam.

Umar added:

"There must be someone freezing tonight. They might be travelers. They might have had to have stopped during the night and set a fire since they were cold. They may need help."

"Yes, maybe," said Aslam.

"Let's take a look," said Umar.

They started off in that direction. It was quite far away, but there might be people in need of help. As they headed towards the place where the fire was set, they conversed. It was getting late and there was no one else on the streets. However, the Caliph and Aslam were walking outside on a cold night. Even though they felt cold, they were happy because they might be able to help people at the end of the journey.

They were getting closer to their destination. They were shocked when they arrived. An elderly woman and a few children surrounded the fire that they had seen in distance. Some water was boiling in a small cauldron over the fire. The children were waiting over the cauldron and frequently checking if it was ready.

The woman and the children did not know the two men who approached them. They were both a little surprised and afraid of their presence. Umar asked the woman:

"May we join you?"

"If you could find a solution to our problem, come over," said the woman.

The woman did not realize that the person, who was visiting them, was the Caliph of the Muslims. After all, it was not easy to guess that he was the Caliph since Umar did not act or dress differently from ordinary people. Umar curiously asked:

"What is the problem?"

"Since we don't have a home, we have to stay outside on this cold night. I set this fire to warm up the children," answered the woman.

"Why are the children crying?" inquired Umar.

"They are hungry. I have nothing to feed them," said the woman.

"What is it that is boiling in the cauldron?" asked the Caliph.

The woman showed them what was inside the cauldron and added:

"Because we do not have anything to cook, I put stones and water inside the cauldron and boiled them. I mix the water occasionally to keep the children busy. I thought that if I delayed them for some time, they would go to sleep. I could not think of any other solution to calm them."

She continued:

"I believe God will hold the caliph Umar accountable for our situation."

Umar was shocked to hear this and asked:

"How do you expect Umar to know of your situation?"

"Why did he want to rule us if he is not supposed to know this?" answered the woman in a sad voice.

These words of the woman shook the Caliph and he asked Aslam to leave. They left the woman and her children immediately. The woman was confused since the two strangers had approached them, listened to their problems and left without saying anything.

The caliph Umar and Aslam went to the food supply depot of the city to get some food for the old woman's family. Umar was touched by the story of the old woman and headed swiftly to the depot. Aslam was having difficulty keeping up with the Caliph. Finally, they got to the depot and put whatever food the woman and children would need into a sack.

Aslam discerned what Umar was about to do. Therefore, Aslam wanted to carry the sack. Yet, Umar prevented Aslam and told him:

"No, Aslam! I should carry this sack."

"I can't let you shoulder this sack. I am your assistant. Please let me do this for you!" insisted Aslam.

But Umar was so determined that he ordered Aslam:

"Put this sack on my shoulder!"

When Aslam insisted:

"How could I let you carry this sack on your shoulder?"

"I am responsible for the well-being of those people. I am the one who is supposed to solve their problems," explained Umar.

The great Caliph carried the sack the entire distance on the cold night and gave it to the family. The children were still waiting for the meal to be ready and the woman seemed even sadder. She continued to mix the water inside the cauldron as she pleaded:

"God will punish Umar for this!"

The old woman and the children were surprised to see Umar and Aslam return. Who were these two men that were visiting them twice that night?

The Caliph put the sack down with the help of Aslam. The fire under the cauldron was fading away. Seeking permission from the old woman, Umar knelt down and reignited the fire. At the same time, Aslam added the wood he had collected. Then, Umar opened the sack and took some food out of it to cook. He was adding more wood under the cauldron as he mixed it to make it cook faster. And finally, the food was ready.

The children did not wait for the food to cool down a bit. The Caliph put some food onto their plates. He invited the timid children to eat, holding their hands. The children were so hungry that as they eat the meal, Umar continued to add more to their plates.

After a while, the children were full and started to play with each other. The woman was so happy. She was thinking, "What would I have done if these men had not come and helped us? How can I thank them?" Turning to Umar, she said:

"You should have been the caliph instead of Umar."

"Why do you think so?" asked the Caliph.

"Because he is not concerned with the problems of his people. But you helped us even though you don't know us."

"Go to the caliph Umar tomorrow and describe your situation. He may put you on a pension and your children will live as happily as their peers do," said the Caliph.

The children fell asleep as they were talking. And the Caliph and Aslam went home feeling content.

The old woman decided to do what the strangers had advised her and she decided to visit the caliph Umar in the morning. As she was on her way to the Caliph, she wondered if he was going to help them. She arrived at the Caliph's office with this concern in her mind. She knocked on the door and entered the room. It was a total surprise! The Caliph was none other than the man who had brought them a sack full of food last night.

The Supporter of the Truthful Is Allah the Almighty

Truthfulness is keeping in mind the benefits of others, bringing them correct information. Being truthful means telling the truth, thinking in the right way, and behaving in the right way. In everything one must say what is right, and even if it is against his own interest or the interest of his relatives.

The sense of confidence provided by being truthful prevents relationships between members of a society from going sour, and prevents solidarity from fading away. The truthful person never contradicts himself. In short, all the psycho-social problems born out of lying are prevented. Truthfulness brings inner peace to all people, and especially to the hearts of the believers. This is because Allah, may His glory be exalted, supports the truthful ones.

A story further illustrates this truth. There was an oppressive governor in the city where Hasan al-Basri used to live. One day, the governor sent his henchmen to apprehend Hasan al-Basri, hoping he would be harmful to him and his cause. In turn, Hasan took refuge in the hut of Habib al-Ajami, with whom he taught for a while in the past. A henchman came in a rage and said:

"Have you seen Hasan al-Basri?"

"Yes."

"Where?"

"Here in my hut."

The men enter the hut. Somehow they cannot find him there. When they come out, they ask again, even more angrily:

"O sheikh, why are telling lies?"

"I have not lied. If you did not see him, what crime did I commit?"

So again they searched the hut. And again they did not find him. When they left, Hasan al-Basri said: "O Habib! I know that, for your sake, my Lord did not show me to them. But why did you tell them about my place? Didn't I have a right of teaching over you?"

Embarrassed, Habib uttered these profound words: "O my teacher! The reason they were not able to find you was not me, but your truthfulness. You know that Allah is the supporter of the truthful. If I told them a lie, they would have taken both of us."

A believer keeps his word, does not betray any trust, does what he must do, fulfills the tasks he shoulders, and gives leadership positions to trustworthy ones. He demonstrates the profound and complete ethics of trustworthiness in his worship and obedience. He is tied to his Lord from the bottom of his heart. He would never venture to be insincere to Him. He would never worship others, and does not cheat in his devotions.

Justice in Islam

Sultan Mehmet the Conqueror declared amnesty after he conquered Istanbul with his army and all prisoners were released except for two Christian priests, who declared that they did not want to be released. These priests were imprisoned by the Byzantine Emperor, because they were advising him to rule justly. Upon this unfair imprisonment the priests vowed not to leave the prison again.

Sultan Mehmet was informed of the situation. He sent two of his soldiers to the prison and invited the priests to the palace. The priests explained to Sultan Mehmet why they did not want to be released. Sultan Mehmet advised the following to these two priests, who were condemning the world:

"I have a suggestion for you. You will travel around our country, where we try to apply the Islamic understanding of justice, and listen to court cases by visiting actual trials. If you come across a similar type of injustice, as you experienced during Byzantine rule, come and report it to me and go back to your prison proving that you are right to isolate yourselves from this unjust world."

The priests found Sultan Mehmet's suggestion very appealing. They immediately started traveling the Muslim country with an official note from the Sultan. Bursa was one of the first stops on the priests' journey. Here is the story of their experience in Bursa:

A Muslim buys a supposedly healthy horse from a Jew. However, as soon as the horse was brought to the Muslim's house, he discovered that it was not well at all. The Muslim could not wait to appeal to the court in the morning. He went up to the judge (*qadi*) of Bursa along with his horse. But the judge was not in the office when he arrived. After waiting for a while, he took his horse back home and the horse died the following night.

The judge, who was informed about the case later on, invited the Muslim man back and told him:

"If I had been in my office when you had first come, you could have turned in the horse that was supposed to be healthy and you would have gotten your money back. But since I was not available in my office at the time, I am responsible for your loss. Therefore, I am going to pay for your loss."

The priests were astonished to see that the judge did not hesitate to pay the compensation out of his own pocket to ensure justice. Then, they headed to another city, İznik, and witnessed another court case:

A Muslim bought a farm from another Muslim and plowed it when the season began. The farmer, who plowed the land with a primitive plow, struck a jar full of gold. He immediately wanted to hand it over to the previous owner of the land and told him:

"I bought the surface of the land but not what resides underneath it from you. If you had known that a jar of gold was buried in your farm, you would not have sold it to me at the same price. That's why you should accept this jar."

But the previous owner of the farm had a different point of view and he explained:

"I think you are wrong in this matter. I sold the land to you including everything that it is composed of. Therefore, I have no right to the gold you found on the land I previously owned. It belongs to you and you are free to spend it however you want."

When the former and current owners of the land could not resolve the dispute over the gold, they appealed to the court. They explained their complaint to the judge and the judge asked them if they had any children. When he heard that one of them had a daughter and the other had a son, the judge suggested that their children get married and that they would receive the gold coins as a dowry.

Upon these two cases that the priests witnessed, they decided that it was pointless to travel across the entire country. They had seen what they needed to see. Thus, they returned to Istanbul and reported the two cases to Sultan Mehmet and added:

"We have come to believe that Islam has a thorough observation of justice and rights. The followers of such a faith could not do any harm to the followers of other faiths. Hence, we changed our minds about secluding ourselves in prison. We believe that no one will be subjected to injustice under your rule."

A Muslim is Trustworthy in His Words and Essence

A Muslim is trustworthy in his words and essence. In order to acquire and maintain it, he makes extra effort and shows extra care. The Messenger of Allah emphasized the inculcation of honesty in children. He particularly checked on parents' relationship with their children and issued general principles.

For instance, no matter what the circumstances are, it is not right for parents to deceive their children, or be apathetic in their dealings with them. Abdullah ibn Amir narrates: "One day, my mother called me. The Messenger of Allah was also sitting in our house. My mother said, 'Come here, I will give you something!' The Messenger of Allah asked my mother: 'What are you going to give him?' Mother replied, 'I will give him a date fruit.' Upon this, our noble Prophet said, 'Know that if you did not give him anything, a sin would have been written down for you.'"

A similar *hadith* was narrated by Abu Hurayra: "The Messenger of Allah said: 'Whoever calls a child by saying 'Come here, I will give you something' and does not do it, there will be a recompense of a sin of lying for that person.'"

A Muslim's essence must be true. Just like his words, he must cleanse his inner world from bad thoughts and sentiments. In other words, a Muslim must speak as he thinks. He must be as he speaks. There should be no discrepancy between his words and his essence. As he becomes a mature believer and earns the trust of others around him, he will inspire confidence in them. How beautifully this *hadith* describes it: "Unless one's heart is right, his belief cannot be right. Unless his tongue tells the truth, his heart cannot be right. One cannot enter Paradise unless one's neighbor feels safe from being harmed." Our dear Prophet advised for the tongue and the heart to be in unison. Both must be on the straight path. When a Muslim's words and essence are right, his work will be right.

In the affairs of Muslims there should be no deception or injustice. Abu Hurayra narrates: "One day, the Messenger of Allah had seen a peck of wheat. When he plunged his hand inside, he noted the surface of the wheat was dry but the bottom was wet. He asked the owner, 'What is this?' The owner replied, 'O Messenger of Allah! It was wetted by the rain.' The Messenger of Allah said: 'Why didn't you place the wet ones on the surface so that people could see them? The one who deceives us is not of us.'"

Thus, the one whose word and essence is right must also be right in his commercial transactions. There is no doubt that when people do business truthfully, this is the mark of their salvation. Abu Said al-Khudri narrates: "The Messenger of Allah said: 'The businessmen who do not deviate from truthfulness and trustworthiness would be together with the Prophets, martyrs and righteous people.'"

Perhaps the most important of all the virtues of that generation—the best of mankind, the Prophet and his Companions—truthfulness was integral to their lives. This honesty established an atmosphere of safety and tranquility in their inner and outer worlds. Abu al-Hawra says: "I asked Hasan, son of Ali ibn Abu Talib, 'What did you learn from the Messenger of Allah?' He said: 'Leave alone anything which gives you doubt, look at the thing which is not doubtful, because truthfulness is closer to the warmer heart, and a lie is closer to doubt.'"

In a similar narration, Sufyan ibn Abdullah al-Thaqafi says: "I asked the Messenger of Allah to tell me about Islam a thing which might dispense with the necessity of my asking anybody after you. He remarked: 'Say I affirm my faith in Allah and then remain steadfast to it.'"

The Rights of Parents

The conduct of the child toward the parents is a right and a duty. That right cannot be compensated, sacrificed to anything, neglected or ignored. As a matter of fact, the Messenger of Allah said, "No child can pay for the rights of the father, unless he finds his father as a slave being sold somewhere, buys him, and emancipates him."

In various *hadiths*, the noble Prophet echoed the sacrifices of mothers. According to a narration by Abu Hurayra: "One day, a person came to the Messenger of Allah and asked him, 'With whom should I spend the most time?' He said, 'Your mother.' The Companion repeated this question exactly three times. He gave the same answer each time. When it was repeated for the fourth time, he answered, 'Your father.'" The Messenger of Allah revealed that the rights of the mother have priority over those of the father.

Fethullah Gülen, in his article "A Tribute to Mothers," touches on this issue with the following statements:

"Think about it, what a long process of preparation they undergo for us, what insurmountable hardships they have come up against and what things they overcome. What challenges they struggle with, and what dreams and weariness they live with. What reveries and dreams their hearts are filled with, and emptied of, what hopelessness and disappointment they suffer. What hardships and burdens they stand firm against and how many ordeals they undergo. What pains they suffer and how they moan. How many times they cry, screaming out and how many times they console our crying. How many times they overflow with compassion and how many times they are in need of compassion. In short, what valuable things they spend for us and what efforts they make, expecting nothing in return.

If there is someone who hugs, cuddles, kisses, and caresses us, who relieves our feelings of sadness and dejection, who shares our worries, who prefers us to eat in her place, us to be dressed well instead of her, who feels her hunger or fullness when we are hungry or full, who bears unimaginable hardships with a super-human effort for the sake of our happiness and joy, who shows us the way for our body to develop, our will to strengthen, for our intelligence to become sharp and perspicacious, for our horizons to be oriented on the Hereafter, a person who does all these with-out expecting-openly or secretly-anything in return, that person is none other than our mother."

The Best Human Being Is a Person Who Could Even Be Friends with Cobras

Fethullah Gülen explains the importance of brotherhood among people who follow the same path: "It is imperative that our friends in this sanctified circle work together in harmony. In the light of the Qur'an's indication and caution: *"We cause you (O humankind) to be a means of testing for one another"* (al-Furqan 25:20) and *"...in order to try you by means of one another"* (Muhammad 47:4) as we are tested with others, we are also tested amongst ourselves. Of course, such testing will earn us different types of Divine rewards.

In this regard, I would say from my perspective, people who have the best manners are those who could even establish rela-tionships with the most cranky by adjusting their behaviors accord-ing to these individuals. Previously, when I explained this topic, I had said: 'The best of human beings are those who could even befriend cobras!'

I ask you, are we lower than Hindu monks that we cannot get along with each other when they could even make friends with cobras! Considering that we are gathered around a sanctified thought.

We are people who should be mannered with the manners of the Messenger of Allah, yet if we are feeling uncomfortable and failing to get along with others due to their oddities, then we need to reexamine our own manners in the treatment room of the conscience. And again, in my perspective, if these people who have dedicated themselves to the service are not getting along with their friends in this sanctified circle, then either they are mental patients or they are egocentrics who victimize others in the lens of their own souls.

So, for the love of God, let us not look for faults in people whom we share the same path, especially in such a time when there is a great need for individuals of all levels and status, in the cause of faith and the Qur'an. Let us not speak against anyone and stop others from speaking behind our brothers. As explained many times before, let us act like prosecutors to our carnal selves and defend others like a lawyer. In this thought, let us all say to ourselves: 'You are a traitor who has released himself to heedlessness. You are a slothful person who cannot leave his house without getting seven hours of sleep. You are a prisoner of the flesh, a slave and servant of your own body.'

Yes, we should always say this and see others as angels. May God soften our hearts and give us success in embracing everyone, beginning with our brothers."

The Passion of Abu Darda for Knowledge

Abu Darda, may Allah be pleased with him, said: "If it were not for these three virtues, I wouldn't have wanted to remain in the world: putting my forehead on the ground in prostration to my Lord, enduring the thirst of fasting during the hottest moments of the day, and spending time with people who sift good words from the bad as one chooses the best of fruits."

This example shows us the kind of God-consciousness of the Companions. Acquiring this *taqwa* is very difficult but not impossible. Fethullah Gülen emphasizes that we must: "...read frequently the books dealing with the lives of the Companions and be decisive to practice what is read. This would help us to be in an atmosphere of spiritual alertness, guiding us in light to the path of the Companions. This is necessary because they are role models for us."

Our noble Prophet likened the Companions to the stars: By coming into their orbit or their sacred attraction, we will reach him. Each one of them is a torch of guidance. It would be impossible to be like them without learning their altruism, their sacrifice, their pain and suffering, and the God-conscious piety enveloping all.

We can have a relationship in our minds with Abdullah ibn Jahsh, Sa'd ibn Rabi, or Ikrima ibn Abu Jahl, in whose life Islam was prevalent for only one and a half years, or ibn Hisham. Their faith and behavior far exceed any human norms. We may say, "I wish I were like Mus'ab, Ibn Jahsh, Hamza, or Ikrima."

When you see some of them while roaming around Hellfire, entering into Islam for a few minutes by saying "Bismillah, ya Allah" (In the Name of Allah, O Allah!) and flying to the summits of Paradise, you will lose yourselves, moaning "I wish..." 'Hopefully these stories will awaken in you a conscience like that of the Companions, and you will be revived by these sentiments.

Most of the Time I Cannot Keep My Chastity and Control My Own Self!

Surely, it is hard to reach that level, especially at the time when unchastity is wide spread and the veil of shame is unveiled. It is quite possible to hear the following words from our youth: "I do not have willpower. That is my problem. Most of the time, I cannot keep my chastity and control my own self. Simply, I plunge into sins. I promised myself not to do it again but, unfortunately, I could not keep my word."

The Sublime Creator gave to his servants, like a drop in the ocean, some of His Attributes and Names. For example, He is the sole Forgiver and we, also, have an attribute of being forgivers to some extent. Likewise, with our human free will, which is a tiny part of the Divine Will, we can enlighten or darken our lives, and choose to be fortunate or not.

Just think about a palace, which is the most magnificent masterpiece of the world. Everything can be found in that palace. Every single pattern of it is in its more beautiful, decorated, precious, modern, and practical state. Electrical and lighting units are incandescent. Imagine that you have a remote control in your hands. And whatever you wish to—just press its "ok" button and it will appear before you. The same case is for electricity, too… if you press "on," then it will be enlightened right away, and by pressing the "off" button, you will darken the entire place.

Behold, you have a remote control of the palace that is as big as this world; and namely that remote control is your willpower. If you say "no" to it, then you will deny such a bounty and accuse the host of the palace. However, if you say that you are using the existing remote control of yours, then it will be a shame on you (and on your magnificent palace).

A mentor of the palace, who said: "Do not let a second look follow the first. The first look is allowed for you but not the second," now is saying to you: "If you use this remote control in an appropriate way, then you will feel comfortable in this palace as well as you will earn many other enormous palaces as gifts of the host." He, the mentor, supported his words with the operation manual of the palace or, let it say, with the sentences of a handbook.

Moreover, in that handbook and in other auxiliary books, it is written that the host of the palace is much closer to you than your jugular vein is, and that despite His immenseness, He is able to have a place in your hearts. Besides, if you do not misuse the remote control, then you will look around with His eyes.

Therefore, instead of saying, "I will not be able to do this or that," or even, "I have a weak mind," we should say: "I have will-power. I just haven't read the existing book till now well and did not obey the mentor of the palace well. From now on, I will use this remote control in an appropriate way for earning thousands of other glamorous palaces. That is why; I will appraise this enormous palace as a remote control of my carnal self." Insomuch, it's our eyes, which we wink with hundreds of times during a day even without realizing that, however now, at least for a few times, we should close our eyes considering that.

A Brave Prophet

A crucial aspect of ethics is courage. A well-mannered individual must be courageous when he needs to be. If he acts timid and cowardly when bravery is required, this is not righteous.

Our glorious Book advises the Messenger to be courageous and decisive: "*So, be patient (O Messenger, with their rejection of faith and with whatever they do), just as those of greatest steadfastness and resolution among the Messengers were patient, and do not seek to hasten (the judgment on) them*" (al-Ahqaf 46:35).

To embody two seemingly opposing virtues is a state only found within a Prophet: to be brave and fearless, and yet, merciful and compassionate. Even Ali—whose battles abound in stories—said: "During the battles when we were squeezed, in trouble somewhere, we would take refuge behind the Messenger of Allah."

The following story illustrates the courage of the Prophet when he met with Ghawrath, an idol worshipper. Jabir reports: "We set out for an expedition towards the Najd. We caught up with the Messenger of Allah at noon in a valley where there was a thick forest and shrubs. The Messenger of Allah sat under a tree to rest. He hung his sword on a branch of the tree. The soldiers, too, lay scattered under the trees to rest in the shade. After a while, the Messenger of Allah called us over. When we approached, he said: 'While I was asleep, a man came and took my sword. At that exact moment, I woke up. He stood before me, my sword in his hand, out of its shield. He intended to kill me with my sword. He asked me, 'Who can save you from me?' And I replied, 'Allah the Almighty.' His sword fell to the ground. It was that man sitting there.' The Messenger of Allah held no grudge against Ghawrath. He wanted no revenge. Ghawrath was the leader of his people. When the Messenger of Allah forgave him publicly, he returned to his men. As he left, he said: 'By Allah, I swear I will join together with any people fighting against you.'"

Another example of unparalleled courage occurred while migrating to Medina. There was a cave on Mount Thawr; it was difficult to climb even by the young. And yet at 53 years of age, the Messenger of Allah climbed briskly to this cave. Meccan polytheists roamed at the mouth of the cave, and Abu Bakr, may Allah be pleased with him, grew concerned for his safety. But the Messenger of Allah showed no change, and with a genuine smile on his lips, he consoled him: "Do not be afraid! Surely, Allah is with us... Abu Bakr, what can befall two who have Allah as the third One with them?"

The Messenger of Allah was a leader. A leader must be a fountain of hope and support for his followers with keen awareness, decisiveness, patience, and fortitude. Consider the observation of Anas about our noble Prophet: "The Messenger of Allah was the most beautiful of human beings, the most generous, and the bravest."

Anas narrates: "One night, people in Medina heard noise and they thought they were under attack. The Prophet mounted a horse that belonged to Abu Talha, bareback, and galloped straight toward the noise, leaving the Medinese behind. Upon his return, he found the people of Medina waiting, their swords on their shoulders. He said: 'There is nothing to be scared of, don't be afraid.' Gesturing to the horse belonging to Abu Talha, which was known for its slowness, he said: 'O Abu Talha! I have found this horse very fast. Afterwards, no horse was able to catch up with it.'"

There are fashions the Prophet does not want his followers to imitate, such as dressing in garments so thin and transparent they show the color of one's skin. One day, the Messenger of Allah saw the sister of Aisha wearing a thin dress. Averting his gaze, he said: "O Asma! After reaching the age of puberty, it wouldn't be right for women to show any part of their body other than this and this." He gestured to her hands and face.

This *hadith* refers to women who cover part of their bodies and leave other parts uncovered. As he advised Asma, our mother of believers, he regarded the nature of all women and desired for women to be sensitive in how they dress.

As it is not legitimate to dress in a way that shows the color of the skin, it is also not appropriate to dress in tight clothes that show the shape of the body. Usama ibn Zayd reported: "The Messenger of Allah gave me the clothes that Dihya al-Kalbi had given to him. I, in turn, gave it to my wife. Then the Messenger of Allah said: 'Tell your wife, not to neglect wearing something underneath, because I am concerned that it would show the shape of her body.'"

Our noble Prophet banned men from dressing like women. Abu Hurayra narrated: "The Messenger of Allah cursed men who dress like women and women who dress like men." Thus, the people who dress like the opposite sex are outside the Divine mercy of Allah the Almighty. Ibn Abbas narrated: "The Messenger of Allah cursed men who try to resemble women and women who try to resemble men."

Perhaps the sensitivity of the Messenger of Allah in this matter aims at warning people not to be trapped in the same ways as those ancient civilizations that acted against the nature of creation, who were annihilated because they drew the wrath of God. A spoiled relationship between genders begins in such behaviors as dressing like the opposite sex, with unavoidable excesses to follow. We must keep our children away from this kind of behavior.

The Qur'an

The Qur'an is a witness proving Allah the Almighty's existence. Everything in this marvelous universe is a sign of creation; the verses of the Qur'an read the universe, and translate it into a language intelligible to humans. The Qur'an discovers hidden treasures as a necessary requirement of the order of causes, within the beautiful Names of the Creator.

The Qur'an is a vehicle to recognize and know the Creator, a key that opens truths, truths hidden by a chain of events among the lines of this universal book. The utterances of the Qur'an are a bright light on true guidance, the source of the light of belief, a key to the treasure troves of meaning and knowledge.

The Qur'an invites people of reflection to look at creatures not for their own sake but to ponder their Creator. The Qur'an is the foundation of *tawhid* with worldly judgments, verdicts, and truths about the unseen world. If we look at the world through the lens of the Qur'an, we may enumerate some of the proofs for God's existence:

Proof of *Inayah* (Grace) and Purpose

The perfect order of the universe shows that the flawless art of creation is displayed and cared for. The obvious wisdom, will and planning of the Creator rejects absolutely the idea of coincidence. Perfection cannot occur without will or choice.

The benevolence and purpose evident in the particles and in the whole universe point clearly to the Divine Being who orders this order; the wisdom and beauty apparent in every creature points back to Divine Essence. He must have superior Attributes, unlimited Knowledge, and infinite Power for the awe-inspiring regularity to be reasonable.

To deny a Creator with superior qualities, means to deny the vast orderliness of the universe, the immense art, and the unending, unequaled beauty of innumerable creatures.

Qur'anic verses refer to the benefits to human beings and other creatures in order to prove their inherent grace and purpose. Verses often say *"Don't they ever think?"* and *"Don't they ever reason?"* and *"Don't you think?"* The Qur'an directs the mind to consult with one's conscience; it speaks simultaneously the mind and heart. If we gaze at the universe with keen awareness in its every particle, in its every move, we would observe traces of unequaled grace. We would find everything has a purpose.

How Should the Young People Convey the Message?

Each Muslim, young or old, has an obligation to pass on the message of God and His Messenger to those around them. This is a duty of utmost priority for all believers. It is for this Divine reason and wisdom that the Prophets were sent. Consequently, we have also been blessed with carrying on this noble duty. In this regard, service is a race of virtue. Those who serve on this path are the most virtuous people on earth.

In this day and age, ideologies and perspectives have been distanced from faith. In fact, faith has been pushed out of daily life. Science and technology are presented as enemies of religion and society is deceived. For this reason, Islam, the Qur'an and issues related to faith should be learned thoroughly and then these Divine lights should be explained to others slowly and with ease.

What Is Representation and Tongue of Conduct?

"Muslim's language used in the process of conveying the truths of religion to others should be the tongue of conduct rather than his physical tongue." (Fethullah Gülen).

Representation and the tongue of conduct means an invitation to religion made by a person, who communicates the message through his or her behavior and good conduct; it is displaying a role model behavior by practicing what is preached. Representation is one the best methods of explaining the truths of religion. One should practice what he attempts to explain to others, at a level which he has benefitted from them. This is an important factor in representation.

True gallantry is in representation. A person who has dedicated himself to explaining the truths of the Qur'an and faith cannot live a life that is contradictory to the realities he explains. Positive behavior and good conduct should be role modeled by those who promote them so that they could have an effect on others. What this means is, a person explaining the Daily Prayers should first offered them himself so that others could say, "Even if this person does not have anything else going for him, his Prayers are enough to prove that he is on the right path." Moreover, even if people do not accept him completely, they should at least believe that Prayers should be taken seriously.

The blessed souls who have undertaken the duty of *irshad* and *tabligh* (guidance and conveying the message) must first practice what they preach. In this regard, the Holy Qur'an cautions us with the following verse: *"Do you enjoin upon people godliness and virtue but forget your own selves, (even) while you recite the Book (and see therein the orders, prohibitions, exhortations and warnings)? Will you not understand and come to your senses?"* (al-Baqarah 2:44). *"O you who believe! Why do you say what you do not do (as well as what you will not do)? Most odious it is in the sight of God that you say what you do not (and will not) do"* (as-Saf 61:2–3).

In one *hadith*, our noble Prophet explains this issue with the following words: "Those who command righteousness to others but forget themselves shall drag their intestines in the hellfire. When they are asked, 'Who are you?' They will reply, 'We are those who commanded righteousness to others but forgot ourselves.'"

The words and attitude of a virtuous person of should complete each other, he should take extreme care in not showing any weakness in his representation and he should first practice what he preaches.

For the Noble Prophet, Representation Came before *Tabligh*

When we analyze the Prophet's life, we see that role modeling was always one step ahead of *tabligh*. He would role model the matters he explained so sensitively that those who observed him would believe in God without having a need for further proof. There were many cases in which people accepted his Prophethood by just looking at him. Abdullah ibn Rawaha says, "Even if he had not come with clear miracles, one look at him would have been enough to believe." What a wonderful way of explaining the truth.

The noble Prophet's representation was so effective that a Jewish scholar, Abdullah ibn Salam embraced Islam with a glance upon his face. He said: "There is no lie on this face. Only a Messenger of Allah can possess such a face."

This means that seeing him was enough to accept him. Those who have dedicated their lives to explaining something to others will know the difficulty of such rapid acceptance. Most of these people work vigorously throughout their lives but cannot find a handful of followers or encourage people to accept their religion by entering their hearts. On the other hand, let us take a look at our noble Prophet. Can you show another person who has established his throne in the hearts of more than one billion people? Or is there another person whose name is chanted out five times a day from the minarets with great excitement and a sound that echoes all over the world?

This means, humanity loves him hence declare their loyalty continuously each day on a number of occasions. Contrary to all, the noble Prophet continues to enter the hearts of people, because he practiced what he preached to others and became a perfect role model for humanity. For this reason, everything he said found a place in the hearts of people and was accepted by nations.

As he invited people to servanthood and obedience to God, he represented this servanthood in its purest form by praying throughout the night until his feet were swollen. One day, he was reminded that all of his past and future sins were already forgiven and asked why he was placing so many burdens upon himself. He replied: "Should I not be a thankful servant?"

If he wished, he could have lived like the kings. Such life of self-indulgence was already offered to him in Mecca. However, for the sake of his religion, he preferred a life of hardship to a life of luxury. It was this simple life style that attracted many people to him.

His Caliph, Umar ibn al-Khattab also lived a very simple life. Yet the life of the Prophet would always bring tears to Umar's eyes. One day, the noble Messenger asked him why he was weeping. Umar replied, "O Messenger of Allah, as the kings of the world sleep in their bird-feathered beds now, you sleep on a mat made up of straws. It has made marks on your body. You are the Messenger of Allah and you deserve a comfortable life more than anyone!" The noble Messenger replied, "O Umar, aren't you satisfied with the world being theirs but the Hereafter ours?"

Yes, he lived a life of simplicity. In other words we could say that he did not live but he let others live. His secret in entering the souls of others lied within the excellence of his representation.

Those who have undertaken the duty of conveying the message have a lot to learn from the behavior and conduct of the noble Prophet. The only condition of conquering the hearts and souls of others is to practice and live everything that is preached, just like the Prophet did.

For example, if a person wishes to explain the beauty of Tahajjud Prayer to others, he must first get up in the middle of the night and offer it by weeping until his Prayer mat is soaked with his tears. Otherwise, he will be slapped with the following verse, "O you who believe! Why do you say what you do not do (as well as what you will not do)?" (as-Saf 61:2). Hence he will never be effective.

The Eminence of Bediüzzaman's Representation

Bediüzzaman, a radiant scholar who has lived every minute of his burdensome life serving the Qur'an and the reality of faith, has conveyed the truths of faith and represented them throughout his life.

After fleeing from captivity in Russia, Bediüzzaman came to İstanbul. An interesting incident occurred during his stay in İstanbul. It was the time of the traditional Kağıthane festival when Bediüzzaman and his three friends, Molla Seyid, Taha and Hacı İlyas, who were members of parliament, got on a small boat. Both sides of Haliç, from the Galata Bridge to Kağıthane were crowded by Greek, Armenian and other women from İstanbul. As they traveled with the boat, they were passing by these women who were celebrating the festival. In his own words, Bediüzzaman was not even aware of this. Molla Taha and Hacı İlyas were checking him out to see if he would look around. After traveling for an hour, they said: "We are amazed at you. You did not even take a glance."

Bediüzzaman replied: "I do not wish for such things because they are unnecessary, transient, sinful pleasures which result in suffering and sorrow."

Bediüzzaman stayed in İstanbul for a total of ten years which consisted of three separate visits. In his own words, he had never glanced at a *haram* once.

When he traveled to Van from Ankara in order to support the National Resistance, a man named Molla Hamid (Ekinci) was at his service. One day, Bediüzzaman said to him: "Just as a small fire could spread to the entire forest and burn it down, so too, looking at *haram* will gradually eat away all the good deeds of a believer. I fear the consequences of such man would be gruesome."

Bediüzzaman was showing great effort and exertion to explain the truths to people through such a high caliber of representation. The biggest impact he made on people was through his tongue of conduct, his manners and representation.

A Man of Representation: Tahiri Ağabey

Bediüzzaman lived a life of self-sacrifice with the utmost determination, a mind-boggling zeal and attitude without making any concessions. Like him, those who studied by his side also became great role models for people around them. From Hulusi Effendi to Hodja Sabri Effendi, from Hafız Ali to Hasan Feyzi Effendi and from Rüşdü Çakın to Mustafa Sungur, all of these giants of righteousness represented the truths to the best of their abilities. On this noble path, they were loyal and faithful. They were the genuine role models of fidelity, faithfulness, representation, the spirit of *tabligh* and devotion.

According to Bediüzzaman's mentality, if there was a student of the *Risale-i Nur* in a certain region, this region was considered to be a conquered in the name of the faith and virtues. Bediüzzaman would consider all individuals who became his students as people who claim: "My support is for my people." The weight of explaining the faith and its truths could only be raised on the shoulders of valiant souls who had locked themselves onto great ideals.

Another brave soul who served Bediüzzaman on this noble path was Tahiri Mutlu. It was a period when the *Risale-i Nur* would be published for the first time and Bediüzzaman sent his students out to find 50–100 liras for the printing costs. He had written *Ayetü'l-Kübra* (The Supreme Sign) but they did not have the funds to publish it.

When Tahiri Mutlu heard this, he said: "Master, give me three days." Then he ran to the village center and announced that everything he possessed was up for sale. This wealth included a rose garden which he had inherited from his grandfather.

A relative who heard this came to him and said: "Tahiri! What are you doing? How will you survive?" He replied: "Why are you worried about my situation? I want to sell the garden, if you are interested then purchase it, if not I will sell it to someone else." His relative gave him the money and purchased the garden with tears pouring out of his eyes. Tahiri Ağabey brought the money to Bediüzzaman and *Ayetü'l-Kübra* was printed with the sacrifice he made.

The devoted generations of today should not fall back in this blessed race hence they should use their freewill in its own rights to keep up with these unique individuals. When any of these individuals traveled to a certain region, a storm erupted there and changes in the name of faith and God began to take place. For this reason, it is important to act in accordance with consistency and by fulfilling the requirements of the freewill. If we show the necessary dedication and effort, God will make this job a part of our nature. In turn, we will stand firmly and upright on our ground without any discouragement.

Owning up to Religion Is a Primary Obligation upon All Believers

In this day and age, supporting religion which means spreading its message is a primary obligation for all believers. No believer is excluded from this imperative duty. Indeed, all believers must learn their religion and put it into practice in their daily lives. And then, they should explain their experiences to others so that the world of others could also be illuminated with *nur* (Divine light).

In all periods of history there have been people who are in need of guidance. Believers traveling on the same boat with those who are wasting their lives in the valleys of misguidance thus looking for a way out, are obligated to fulfill their responsibilities towards their co-travelers. Besides being a mission given by God himself, this duty is also a prerequisite of being human. Depending on their status, level and means available, everyone has an obligation towards this duty. Otherwise, being accountable for this duty on the Day of Judgment will be a difficult task.

When we scrutinize the history, we will see that those who have undertaken this noble duty of invitation and guidance have always followed the same path. After receiving this noble duty, the Messenger of Allah spent every day of his life conveying the message of religion. He would travel door to door looking for a friendly face and a heart to convey his message.

Initially, no one showed any consideration or interest. Later, some began to ridicule him. Gradually, their attitudes turned to harassment, insult and torture. They were laying thorns on his path and pouring the internal organs of dead animals down his head as he stood for the Prayer. They believed that it was ok to torture and harass the Messenger of Allah in all forms of manner. However, contrary to all attacks, the noble Messenger did not give an inch and never felt wearisome of his duty, because this was the very reason for his existence. He visited everyone repeatedly, including his archenemies. He conveyed the Divine message. Who knows how many times he visited Abu Jahl and Abu Lahab, archenemies of Islam and faith, and delivered the message of Islam to them! He was walking around the fairs and visiting all the tents with an intention to save the faith of one person. Wherever he went, doors would be shut on his face yet he would go again and again with the same message.

As Mecca became an unlivable place for the noble Messenger, he migrated to Medina. He was to spread his Divine light in this city now.

He did not stay away from his duty of invitation and guidance, not even for a moment. He explained religion to the smallest detail and invited people to it. Throughout his stay in Medina, even during the conflicts, he did not withdraw from conveying his message to every individual.

Our noble Messenger was a unique individual who carried the weighty obligation of Prophethood on his shoulders for twenty-three years, fulfilling his responsibilities like no other man of action.

If You Are Saying It, Then Do It

A person's value by the side of God and his effectiveness in public is proportional to his abstinence from what is prohibited by God and fulfillment of the religious obligations. Words and actions are the two important languages of explaining and spreading the truths of faith. This sole language which appears to be two-sided can produce amazing results if it is correctly implemented. The marks left by those who do not fall into contradiction with their words and actions will be lasting.

A person who sleeps through the night with lassitude should be ashamed to talk about the *Tahajjud* (the Night) Prayer. If he is not offering his Prayers in serenity and tranquility, then he should refrain from defining a perfect Prayer. The effectiveness of the topics that relate to God depends on the practices of the individual who explains them.

However, the verse, *"O you who believe! Why do you say what you do not do (as well as what you will not do)? Most odious it is in the sight of God that you say what you do not (and will not) do,"* (as-Saf 61:2–3) should not be misunderstood. When the verse asks "why", it is not implying that you should not say what you do not do. What it is actually saying is: "Since you are saying it then you should be doing it." So, saying something and not doing it draws the punishment of God. This means that the verse is not suggesting that one shouldn't say the things he does not do himself, but it is indicating that one should be determined to practice what he preaches.

Some Companions who had similar concerns about the issue asked the noble Prophet. Anas ibn Malik explains: "We asked the Prophet of God: "O Messenger of Allah, should we not encourage people to do good and prevent them from doing evil, if we are not practicing everything perfectly?" The noble Prophet replied:

"No! Even if you do not practice everything perfectly, you should still invite others to good and if you are not able to protect yourselves from all the unlawful things, you should still prevent others from doing evil.

Conveying the message and practicing the religious obligations are two different forms of worship. If you abandon both, you are committing two sins, but if you abandon one, you are committing one sin hence you are confining yourself to ineffectiveness. Saying what you do not do or not practicing what you are saying will draw the Divine punishment and it will break the power of effectiveness. Furthermore, it will have a negative impact on your credibility and your words will have no effect thus they will be forgotten very quickly.

What Does "Fana fi'l-Ikhwan" Mean?

It is an indispensable sentiment that needs to exist between the members of an ideology which seeks to achieve genuine brotherhood. Bediüzzaman who describes this sentiment as "annihilating yourself between your brothers and preferring their souls over yours" has introduced the term *fana fi'l-ikhwan* into our literature. *Fana fi'l-ikhwan* is a condition in which individuals reach complete perfection in love where they willingly sacrifice all bounties, material and spiritual by preferring other's to their own souls. In short, this condition is defined as *tafani* which means individuals annihilating themselves in one another. Bediüzzaman explains this with the following words:

"As if it were you who possess the merits and virtues of your brothers and sisters, take pride in them and be thankful to God for them.

The Sufis circulate among themselves such terms as 'annihilation in the guide,' and 'annihilation in the Messenger.' I am not a Sufi, but we should have this principle among ourselves as 'annihilation in the brothers and sisters.' This is called among the brothers and sisters 'mutual annihilation.' It means the brothers and sisters being annihilated in one another. That is to say, oblivious of their own merits and the pride which may arise from them, each person lives with the merits and feelings of their brothers and sisters in their mind. The basis of our way is brotherhood."

"Our way is also the closest friendship. Friendship requires being the closest, most self-sacrificing friend, the most appreciative companion, and the most magnanimous brother or sister."

Certainly, a friendship which originates from the light of faith and flourishes with the flowers of *iman* and takes the transient human being to eternity cannot be compared with any other earthly friendships. *"Those who are intimate friends (in the world) will be enemies one to another on that Day, except the God-revering, pious"* (az-Zukhruf 43:67).

Indeed, those who befriend each other for worldly reasons will leave their friendship on earth when they go. Sometimes, such friendships do not even last on earth. However, friendships formed for God continues on earth and in the life after. Another thing faith gives to humanity is the pure brotherhood that strengthens the bridge between the temporary and the eternal realms. Believers are those who love only for God and condemn only for God. On the Day of Judgment, our Lord will give good news to believers who have organized their lives in accordance with the conditions of brotherhood described above hence prepared themselves for the Hereafter: *"O My servants! You will have no fear today, nor will you grieve!"* (az-Zukhruf 43:68).

Is the good news of this Divine revelation not worth enduring the burdens that come from our brothers in this short life? Is it not worth taking our time to correct the mistakes of our brothers? Or, is it not worth refraining from insignificant rivalries on the road to our true goal? It is worth the trouble a hundred times over! Let us listen to Bediüzzaman: "O my brothers and sisters! Our way which we try to follow in the service of the wise Qur'an is based on truth and requires true brotherhood. Brotherhood requires self- annihilation among the brothers and sisters and preferring them to oneself. Therefore, there should not be rivalry among us that arises from seeking status in people's eyes."

The reason for this is, just as *iman* gives life to the heart, brotherhood in religion gives life to society. Bediüzzaman presented *fana fi'l-ikhwan* as a principle of life and emphasized the significance of this mutual support between brothers with the following words:

Life is the product of unity and oneness. When harmonious unity departs, so does the spiritual life. As the Divine verse indicates, the congregation loses its jubilation in the absence of order: *"And obey God and His Messenger, and do not dispute with one another, or else you may lose heart and your power and energy desert you; and remain steadfast. Surely, God is with those who remain steadfast"* (al-Anfal 8:46).

"If three 1's do not unite or come together, they will have only the value of 3. But if they unite or come together, they will gain the value of 111. Four separate 4's make 16. But if they come together in true brotherhood, along the same line for the fulfillment of the same duty, they will have the value of the power of 4444. History records numerous events which bear witness to the fact that 16 self-sacrificing people in true brotherhood have obtained the moral strength of more than 4000 people."

The difference between unity and disunity is quite obvious for all of us. However, knowing something and practicing it are different things. The believers know the necessity of helping each other, sharing the workload of servanthood, mutual support on the path of righteousness and the importance of refraining from disunity due to personal gains. However, implementing it and making a decision on how to protect themselves from conflicts is not that easy.

In response to faith, one should also uncover the secrets of behaving without falling into the tricks of the devil and following the temptations of the world and the carnal desire. This secret is: preferring your brother over yourself; choosing sincerity over rivalry and the Hereafter over worldly contentment. In relation to this, Bediüzzaman says: "Prefer the souls of your brothers and sisters to your own in honor, position, public approval, and even in things like the material benefits of which the carnal soul is enamored."

On another occasion, he states: "Do not open the doors of criticism to each other. There are many things to be criticized outside the circle of your brotherhood. Just as I feel proud of the qualities you possess, feel happy that you have them and also consider them to be mine, you should also evaluate each other as the way your master does. Each one of you should be a promoter of the other's virtues.

The Companions Were Racing with Each Other in Altruism

The Companions who were taught by the noble Prophet had also displayed an inimitable spirit of altruism as they lived exemplary lives. In every period of their lives they had shown an effort and exertion with feelings of altruism as they left behind their homes, families, wealth, work and dignity, when it was necessary, to defend the security and unity of Muslims.

Within the Companions, one of the altruistic souls who hold a special place is Abu Talha al-Ansari. He is a Companion well known for his altruism in the name of God. As much as being an altruist, he was also a brave soldier who defended the Prophet with his life during the battle of Uhud. He was a great archer who formed a living shield in front of the Prophet at Uhud. As he did this, he shouted "Do not worry, O Messenger of Allah, they cannot harm you before they martyr me." In turn, the noble Messenger honored him with the following words, "Within the army, the roar of Abu Talha is more blessed than a thousand men."

Abu Talha and his wife Umm Sulaym had a different place in the heart of the noble Messenger of Allah. He would visit this family frequently and honored them. They would offer him whatever they had in their house. The noble Prophet had a share of whatever that was cooked in this house. Their behavior showed that they were kind, sensitive individuals who understood people's situations and displayed an exemplary altruism by sharing whatever they had.

The first addresses of Islam were the Companions of the Messenger of Allah; therefore, their attitudes towards the revelation and the *hadith* were quite important from the point of comprehending and practicing the Divine commandments and the message of the noble Prophet, and also from the perspective of becoming role models for the following generations. In this regard, Talha was a perfect example for the following generations. The reason for this is he had comprehended the messages that invited him to altruism and implemented them in a most beautiful way.

According to Anas ibn Malik, Talha was the wealthiest person amongst the *Ansar* of Medina. His favored property was the garden of Bayruha which was located across the Masjid an-Nabawi (the Prophet's Mosque). The Messenger of Allah would frequently visit this garden and drink from the sweet water there.

When the verse, *"You will never be able to attain godliness and virtue until you spend of what you love (in God's cause, or to provide sustenance for the needy). Whatever you spend, God has full knowledge of it"* (Al Imran 3:92) was revealed, Abu Talha came to the noble Messenger and said: "O Messenger of Allah; God says that unless we give what we love the most, we cannot become righteous. I love my garden Bayruha and I am giving it away as a charity. O Messenger of Allah, make use of it for the sake of God. The noble Messenger replied: "Well done Abu Talha! This is a profitable deal. I heard what you said but I suggest that you leave this property to your relatives." Abu Talha said: "I will do this O Messenger of Allah." He then distributed the property amongst his relatives and his cousins.

As it is seen, our Prophet was quite pleased by the fact that he had taken the message of the verse and displayed his altruism accordingly.

Abu Hurairah explains that one day a man came to the Prophet and said: "I am hungry." The noble Messenger sent a message to one of his wives and requested something to eat. His wife replied: "O Messenger of Allah, there is nothing but water in the house." The Messenger of Allah then requested the same thing from his other wife, she replied the same way: "By the One who sent you as a Messenger, there is nothing but water in the house!" Upon hearing this, the noble Prophet addressed his Companions and said: "Who would like to invite this person to their house tonight?" A person from the *Ansar* said: "I can take him as a guest O Messenger of Allah! Then he took the poor person to his house. As he entered the house, he asked his wife: "Is there anything to eat?" His wife replied: "No, there is only enough food for the children." The Companion said to his wife: "Put the children to bed. Then turn off the oil-lamp when the guest comes into the room. We will sit down and pretend that we are eating as well." The guest ate while they went to bed with empty stomachs. The next morning when that Companion came to the Masjid an-Nabawi, our noble Prophet said to him: "God was pleased with what you have done for your visitor last night."

In another narration of this *hadith*, there is an indication that the following verse was revealed after the incident:

> Those who, before their coming, had their abode (in Medina, preparing it as a home for Islam and faith, love those who emigrate to them for God's sake, and in their hearts do not begrudge what they have been given; and (indeed) they prefer them over themselves, even though poverty be their own lot. (They, too, have a share in such gains of war.) Whoever is guarded against the avarice of his own soul—those are the ones who are truly prosperous. (al-Hashr 59:9).

The society needs people who are unselfish, altruist and ready to share whatever they have at all times. Such people should be praised and valued by the society.

Consultation Is the Commandment of the Qur'an

Luqman the Wise says: "Before doing something, consult someone who has done it before, because, he will give his opinion to you for free on matters that may have cost him dearly." No matter how smart a person is, he is on the wrong path unless he consults others in relation to solving issues. Even our noble Prophet, who was the smartest of all human beings, solved issues through consultation. There are many examples of this during the Age of Happiness:

During the battle of Badr, our noble Prophet wanted to camp near the closest water wells. Al-Hubab ibn al-Mundhir came to him and said: "O Messenger of Allah! Did you choose this place because God has commanded it hence we are not permitted to go any further? Or is it just a part of your battle strategy?"

"No, it is just an opinion, a battle strategy," replied the noble Prophet.

"O Messenger of Allah, then this is not a good place to camp! We should go to the wells that are closest to the enemy.

Then, we should make a small pool there and destroy the other wells so that the enemy does not benefit from them."

The Messenger of Allah replied: "This is a good idea." Then he did what the Companion suggested.

Yes, consultation is the commandment of the Qur'an and thus it is a form of worship. Those who have chosen the truths of the Qur'an as a guide to themselves must obey its commandments and deal with their issues through consultation.

Consultation also means that human beings need each other. In other words, they are a group of people who love, respect and need each other; therefore, they value each other's opinion and they accept the notion of consultation as a fundamental principle amongst themselves and hence act accordingly.

A person, who does not consult with people of experience, does not love his colleagues. Moreover, it means he does not value the views of others because he believes his opinion is always better than the opinion of others.

Since we cannot think of a person who does not need anyone, a person who refrains from consultation is an individual who is oblivious of his own nature which is based on impotence, deficiency and destitution. Such attitude is quite dangerous for a human being. Giving importance to consultation does not come from deficiency but it originates from maturity and the thought of doing a better service.

Supererogatory (*Nawafil*) Prayers

In addition to the Sunnah of the five Prescribed Prayers, there were also Prayers that the Prophet performed on a regular basis. These Prayers are called supererogatory Prayers— Prayers that are the means of becoming spiritually closer to the Creator. These are some of the optional Prayers:

Tahajjud Prayer

Tahajjud is a supererogatory Prayer performed after the Night Prayer and having slept a while. Therefore, it can be performed in the early, middle, or latter part of the night until the Morning Prayer. This is a prayer that the Prophet performed on a regular basis, a Prayer that bears great reward. Tahajjud may be executed by performing the minimum two and maximum eight units of Prayer. Giving *salam* at the end of performing every two units of Prayer is greater in reward. In one of the *hadith* the noble Prophet said: "Observe the Tahajjud Prayer, for it was the practice of the righteous before you; it is the means of coming closer to your Lord, an expiation for your evil deeds, and a shield against sin."

Duha (Forenoon) Prayer

This supererogatory Prayer is performed between the period after the sun has fully risen in the morning and until thirty minutes before the time for noon prayer begins. Duha Prayer is performed by praying at least two or at the most twelve units of Prayer. Referring to the Duha Prayer, the Messenger of Allah said: "Whoever observes the Duha (Forenoon) Prayer, with the exception of the rights of others, will be forgiven for all sins even if they are like the foam of the ocean."

Awwabin Prayer

The Awwabin Prayer is an optional form of worship. The word *awwabin* means those who turn to God frequently in Prayer. This is the minimum of two and the maximum six units of Prayer, performed after the Evening Prayer.

Tasbih Prayer

The Prayer of Tasbih (glorification) consists of four units, in which Al-Fatiha and some more verses of the Qur'an are recited in every unit of the Prayer. On completion of the recitation of Al-Fatiha and additional verses of the Qur'an in the first unit, "Subhanallahi walhamdulillahi wala ilaha illallahu wallahu akbar" is recited fifteen times while in the standing position. The same *tasbih* is recited ten times in the bowing position, and then rising from the bowing position is recited another ten times while standing. The individual then prostrates and repeats the *tasbih* ten times while prostrating, and again in the sitting position, and another ten times in prostration, then rising to the sitting position again recites the *tasbih* another ten times thus completing the first unit of the Prayer. The remaining units are performed in the same manner until the completion of all four units of the Prayer.

In addition to the supererogatory Prayers stated above, there are also various supererogatory Prayers performed on the eclipse of the sun and moon, during times of drought and disaster, after performing ablutions, on entering the mosque, and during the times of difficulty.

Reading Brings Renewal

In the flow of life, anyone, may wither and live without enthusiasm from time to time. But remaining alive is one of the duties of the believer. It is unavoidable for one without a fresh influx to become brittle and lifeless, like a tree without water. No matter what stage of life one is in, one must produce something, and one's action is directly proportional to one's reading. To be up and running, to have forward momentum and action, depends on reading.

A believer reads to retain his liveliness. The readings will be constant and regular. For those who share the same goals, coming together and discussing books will increase the benefits. Those people who renew themselves and strengthen their faith within the written word will be firmer in their resistance against withering.

Perhaps it is possible to escape the suffocating atmosphere of over-familiarity by reading something less customary, such as the sacred lives of those Companions who wrote their names in golden letters on the pages of history. Perusing the golden pictures of their lives, while escaping from the enticing, poisonous beauty of this transient world, and pouring the truth of what we read into those who thirst, we will restore our balance through reading.

People Should Say "There Is No Lie on This Face"

In this day and age some people, who are hungry for our religion, stay away from it because of the un-Islamic attitudes and behaviors of some Muslims. There are many examples of this. Here is one example:

During Ramadan, the people of a village in Erzurum organized a sermon to be delivered by İbrahim Hakkı, a renowned scholar of the era. They paid money to a non-Muslim individual who worked as a servant to pick the Imam with his horse and bring him to the village. The non-Muslim servant arrived to the house of the Imam but there was only one horse. So the Imam decided to take turns in riding the horse, just as Umar did when he traveled to Jerusalem with his servant. The servant tried to refuse the offer arguing that the villagers would be upset with him but the Imam insisted: "Son, we do not know what will happen to us at the time of our last breath. You are worried about the admonishment of the villagers yet I am worried about the Judgment Day when I shall stand before God and answer for my life on earth." The imam would not take no for answer, he had already made his mind up.

As Divine wisdom decided, when they were about to enter the village, just like in the case of Umar, it was the servant's turn to ride the horse. The servant was afraid of the villagers so he decided to give up on his right to mount the horse. He requested that İbrahim Hakkı remained on the horse as they entered the village. However, the Imam insisted: "It is your turn to ride the horse!"

He entered the village walking in front of the horse. As the villagers saw this, they gathered around the servant and began to scream at him: "How could you be so disrespectful? Shame on you! You let an old scholar walk when you ride the horse in your young age. Is this your loyalty? Did we ask you to do this?"

However, they stopped harassing the young man when İbrahim Hakkı explained the arrangement them made between them. At that moment one of the villagers approached the non-Muslim servant and said: "You have seen the level of virtue here. Why don't you become a Muslims?"

After a few moments of consideration, the servant made the following noteworthy statement: "If you are inviting me to your religion, I will never accept! But if you are talking about the religion of this old man, I have already embraced it during our journey."

Yes, a person of *tabligh* should be so sensitive that for the sake of God, the Prophet, his religion and his people, he should let others claim: "There is no lie on this face." People who look at him should reach the following conclusion: "If it is his religion that gives him such perfect manners and a dignified character then there could be no lie in this religion either."

Altruism in This Day and Age

The last century was a period in which calamities, disasters and catastrophes have rained upon our people. It would be difficult to show another era in which so many calamities piled up one after the other on a same nation or society. More than ever, the people of today need the truth, reality and the sound of Qur'anic breaths. Consequently, people who are going to undertake this task should be extremely self-sacrificing thus they should attend to the problems of our people just like a compassionate doctor and with great understanding of servanthood.

If the example is suitable, a great ship has been aground. There is a need for enormous support and self-sacrifice so the ship could set sail again. Every ideology needs support and self-sacrifice that is proportional to its greatness and value. The self-sacrifice required of the movement depends on the enormity and greatness of the ideal. That is to say, if the level of self-sacrifice is kept at the same level as the previous centuries, we will not accomplish what is expected of us. A required service can only be achieved if the level altruism is kept above the normal, just like the sacrifice made by the Companions of the Prophet.

Our faith requires the self-sacrifice from us today. Praise be to God that many incidents of altruism which reminds us of the Companions are also witnessed today, hence this gives us hope for the future. Fethullah Gülen talks about one of these incidents during his sermon: "There was a man who used to sell *lahmajun* (Turkish pita made with mincemeat). He was a self-sacrificing soul who came to me about two years ago and said: "My respected teacher, you are looking for a place where students could stay. I have bought two houses by working with this pushcart stall as I sold *lahmajun* on the streets for many years. One of these houses is enough for me. If you accept, I like to give the other one for student accommodation."

I could not refuse such an offer made with an intention to please God. I hoped that by accepting, my Lord would also forgive me using his altruism as an intercession.

This person who had given his heart to God did not stop there. He was hungry for good deeds. A six or seven months later, he came back again and said: "My respected teacher, there is a big garden in front of my house, I want to build a boarding school there and accommodate one hundred students."

I looked at the face of this man who sold *lahmajun* in the streets with a small pushcart and in bafflement I asked: "How are you going to build a boarding school by selling *lahmajun* on the streets?"

He replied: "Do not worry; with your prayers and the blessing of God, I shall accomplish this."

He did what he said and by selling *lahmajun* from that small pushcart, he built a boarding school. Obviously, he had made great sacrifices from his personal life in order to save this kind money. A friend of mine had seen his shoes one day and realized that they were unwearable. He told him he needed a pair of used shoes and asked if anyone had a pair. This was a man who had sacrificed himself to the truth and given his heart to God. This is how a true altruist was supposed to be.

It is the responsibility of the people of faith to spread the truths of faith. This duty is a cause bigger and more important than any issue on earth. This is why a believer must make time to worship, serve faith, and to discipline his soul with knowledge.

Moreover, he should spend his time on guiding and inviting the new generation to a virtuous life through discipline and practice. This should be done with extreme care, interest and strength. Believers should consider the superfluous things which are seen as beauties by worldly people as meaningless hence they should not waste their time with them.

How fortunate are those who consider the life-style of the indecent people which is embellished on the outside but filthy in the inside, pretty on the outside and decomposed in the inside, as nothing but meaningless fun and games hence they do not feel any interest towards them and ruin their eternal contentment. A thousand greetings to those who sacrifice their time for building an "Age of Happiness" for future generations and for a cause that promises eternal happiness.

The Scholars Placed Emphasis on the Night Prayers

Scholars write that people who overeat in the evening must not sleep before melting away the excess food through *dhikr*, the recitation of the Qur'an, and repentance. Sheikh Abdulqadr al-Jilani advises reciting the following verses and prayers just before sleeping, to help us awaken easily at dawn: three *istighfar* (repentance), the first ten and the last ten verses of the *surah* al-Kahf, the last two verses of the *surah* al-Baqarah, and the *surah* al-Kafirun, and then this prayer: "My God, wake me up at an hour which is pleasing to You. Make use of me in the things which would bring me closer to You and move me away from Your wrath. O my Lord! I ask of You, grant me my requests, I desire Your forgiveness, forgive me, I am praying to You, accept my prayers!"

Muadha al-Adawiyyah was among those who spent the night in devotion. Even on cold nights she wore thin clothes so that she would not fall asleep. When night came she said, "This is my last night!" and began to recite her prayers. When she felt sleepy, she would roam the room and say: "O carnal soul! Sleep is before you. After death, you will sleep a long time, either in pain or in joy."

They Led Their Lives in Devotion to Allah

Thanks be to God, our history is full of friends of Allah who we may use as role models. One is Mansur ibn Mu'tamir. Ijli narrates: "Mansur ibn Mu'tamir was from the successors of the successors. One of his neighbors was a woman who lived with her daughter. When it became dark, the mother and daughter used to climb the flat roof of the house to sleep, and when it became dawn, they came down.

· Under darkness, the daughter used to see a column on her neighbor's roof. When Mansur died, the daughter asked: "My dear mother, what happened to the pillar on the roof of our neighbor's home?" The mother replied: "My daughter, it was not a pillar, it was the head of the household, Ibn Mu'tamir, and he died!" Because every night he stood there to pray, she thought he was a pillar. This is not an isolated event; there are similar reports about people like Aswad ibn Yazd al-Nakhai.

One of the rarest women in the world, Rabia al-Adawiyyah, got up at night and worshiped her Lord in a remote place, saying, "My Lord! Friends have found friends, and I have come to you!" Expecting nothing, just to obtain His pleasure, she tied her hands before Him to worship Him alone.

The Spirit of Responsibility Should Always Be Kept Alive

When people utter the words "Why should I bother with this", a dialogue that took place between Sultan Süleyman the Magnificent and Yahya Effendi, who was an important scholar of the era, comes to mind. The Sultan and Yahya Effendi are milk-brothers. Yahya Effendi is a saintly individual whose prayers were potent.

One day, Sultan Süleyman ponders about the future of the Ottoman State and writes a letter to Yahya Effendi: "My dear brother, you are a scholar of wisdom. Bless us with your knowledge and tell us what will become of the sons of Uthman."

Yahya Effendi replies with the following message: "Why should I bother with this, brother?"

Sultan Süleyman was stunned by the reply hence quickly he decided to visit Yahya Effendi at his dervish lodge in Yıldız Park. He was disappointed at the fact that no answer was given to his question. As the Sultan walked in he asked, "Dear brother, you have not answered my question, have I done something wrong?"

Yahya Effendi replied, "I have answered your question, yet I am surprised that you failed to understand."

"What did it mean?" asked Sultan Süleyman.

Yahya Effendi replied: "My brother, in a nation, if injustice and tyranny becomes wide-spread and if those who see this say "Why should I bother with this" and do not act; if a sheep is consumed by the shepherd instead of a wolf and if those who know do not say anything; if the screams of the poor and the innocents rise to the sky and if no one hears them, then wait for the demise of you nation. Your treasures will be looted and your soldiers will rebel, this is the time of the end."

Fortunate are those who are aware of their humanity and possess exalted feelings of responsibility. They could never say, "Why should I bother with this." When they behold a bleeding wound, they do not ignore this as their hearts burn with agony. They feel ashamed before God and their conscience feel the pressure of the Prophet's spirituality hence they do not leave unguarded the sanctified cause which was entrusted upon them.

We Have Also Accepted the Resignation of Those Who Have Given Their Resignation to You!

Great poet Mehmet Akif Ersoy would frequently attend the Sultan Ahmed Mosque for the Morning Prayers. Each time he went to the mosque, he saw an old man weeping in the corner. One day, the old man explained his story to Akif and he was deeply affected. Later, Akif explained the conversation he had with the old man:

"Every day I would perform the Morning Prayer at Sultan Ahmed. No matter how early I went there, I would see an old man sitting at the corner of the Mosque and weeping continuously. His hair and beard had completely turned gray and the old man looked extremely sad and hopeless. He cried so much that I did not witness a minute in which he did not weep. I could not help myself but wonder as to why this man wept so much. One morning, I approached him and asked, "Why are you weeping so much? Should a man lose hope from the mercy of God?" He glanced at me with his aged eyes and replied:

"Do not make me explain. My heart is about to explode." I continued to insist and finally he began to explain his story: "Dear sir, I was a major in the army during the rule of Sultan Abdülhamid. I had a military unit under my command. I served in the army until my parents passed away. Following their deaths, I decided to resign from active duty. I had inherited a significant amount of wealth. In order to supervise this wealth, so that it was not misused, I decided to give in my resignation. I wrote a request for my resignation and sent it to the royal authority. In my request letter I had written, "Both my parents have passed away. We have a significant amount of wealth and properties at various locations. Consequently, someone needs to attend to our businesses and properties. Please consider my situation when deciding on my resignation."

A few days later, I received a letter from the Sultan himself. I opened the letter with great enthusiasm. The Sultan was informing me that my resignation was not accepted. It was obvious that they had given my resignation request letter to the Sultan himself. I wrote another letter and reapplied for it. There was no change in the decision. Finally, I decided to visit the Sultan in person and ask for my resignation. Sultan Abdülhamid was a courageous individual. Sometime ago, I worked with his personal assistant. He explained a few things about the Sultan: "When Abdülhamid traveled in his carriage, people sitting on his left and right would be afraid to even breathe."

Abdülhamid was a saintly person. For this reason, I decided to explain my situation to this majestic and heroic man in person, may God have mercy on his soul. I visited him and said:

"O Sire, I urge you to accept my resignation, this is my situation." He paused for a few minutes. I could tell from his expression that he did not wish to accept my resignation. For this reason I became a bit more adamant. Upon my persistence, he turned towards me and with anger he said "Your resignation has been accepted" as he made a push-away gesture with the back of his hand.

I was happy about the result. Quickly, I returned to my town and took control over my businesses. One night, I saw an incredible dream. In the realm of metaphysics all the Muslim armies had gathered for inspection. Our regiments fighting in the east and the west were being inspected by the Messenger of Allah, himself.

Our noble Prophet was standing in front of the Yıldız Palace and the entire army was marching through in total discipline as they saluted him. There were prominent Ottoman Sultans besides him and Abdülhamid was also there. The Sultan was standing behind the Prophet in a respectful manner. As the army marched through, the regiment that I used to command appeared. It did not have a commander hence the soldiers were walking in an undisciplined manner.

Upon seeing this, the noble Prophet turned to Abdülhamid and said: "O Abdülhamid, where is the commander of this regiment?"

Abdülhamid replied in humility: "O Messenger of Allah, the commander of this regiment resigned. He insisted so much that we gave him the permission to resign."

The noble Prophet said: "We have also accepted the resignation of those who have given their resignation to you!"

The old man concluded his story with the words, "Now tell me, should I stop crying or not?"

Indeed, the noble Prophet is behind every step that is taken in the name of God. If a believer wishes to see the Prophet's support then he should fulfill his duty accordingly.

Qualities of a *Hizmet* (Service) Devotee

In one of his articles, Fethullah Gülen summarizes the qualities of the people who have devoted themselves to *Hizmet* (a word of Arabic origin, used in Turkish to mean disinterested, voluntary and beneficial service to others):

1. People of service must resolve, for the sake of the cause to which they have given their heart, to cross over seas of "pus and blood."

2. When they attain the desired object, they must be mature enough to attribute everything to its Rightful Owner, and be respectful and thankful to Him. Their voices and breaths glorify and magnify God, the Sublime Creator. Such people hold everyone in high regard and esteem, and are so balanced and faithful to God's Will that they do not idolize those whom they praise for their services.

3. First of all, they understand that they are responsible and answerable for work left undone, must be considerate and fair-minded to everyone who seeks their help, and must work to support the truth.

4. They are extraordinarily resolved and hopeful even when their institutions are destroyed, their plans upset, and their forces routed.

5. People of service are moderate and tolerant when they take new wings and once again soar to the summits, and so rational and wise that they admit in advance that the path is very steep. So zealous, persevering, and confident are they that they willingly pass through all the pits of hell encountered on the way.

6. So sincere and humble are such people that they never remind others of their accomplishments.

ANSWERS

Chapter 1
1. A 2. C 3. B 4. B 5. D 6. A 7. B 8. A

Chapter 2
1. D 2. D 3. C 4. D 5. A 6. B 7. C

Chapter 3
1. C 2. A 3. B 4. C 5. A 6. D 7. B

Chapter 4
1. A 2. C 3. B 4. C 5. A 6. A 7. D 8. B 9. C

Chapter 5
1. A 2. C 3. C 4. D 5. D 6. A 7. B 8. B 9. A

Chapter 6
1. A 2. B 3. A 4. C 5. B 6. C 7. D 8. C

Chapter 7
1. A 2. C 3. B 4. A 5. B 6. C 7. B 8. D 9. A

Chapter 8
1. B 2. A 3. C 4. A 5. C 6. B 7. B 8. C 9. D 10. C

Chapter 9
1. D 2. C 3. B 4. C 5. A 6. C 7. D 8. B 9. A 10. D

Chapter 10
1. D 2. C 3. B 4. C 5. A